# THE HUMOROUS MAGISTRATE (OSBORNE)

THE MALONE SOCIETY
REPRINTS, VOL. 178
2011 (2012)

PUBLISHED FOR THE MALONE SOCIETY
BY MANCHESTER UNIVERSITY PRESS

Oxford Road, Manchester M13 9NR, UK
and Room 400, 175 Fifth Avenue, New York, NY 10010, USA
www.manchesteruniversitypress.co.uk

*Distributed exclusively in the USA by*
Palgrave, 175 Fifth Avenue, New York,
NY 10010, USA

*Distributed exclusively in Canada by*
UBC Press, University of British Columbia, 2029 West Mall,
Vancouver, BC, Canada V6T 1Z2

*British Library Cataloguing-in-Publication Data*
A catalogue record for this book is available from the British Library

*Library of Congress Cataloging-in-Publication Data applied for*

ISBN 978-0-7190-8701-1

*Typeset by New Leaf Design, Scarborough, North Yorkshire*

*Berforts Information Press Ltd, Oxford*

This edition of *The Humorous Magistrate* was prepared by Jacqueline Jenkins and Mary Polito, and checked by N. W. Bawcutt.

The Malone Society is grateful to the University of Calgary for permission to publish this edition of the manuscript of *The Humorous Magistrate*: University of Calgary, Osborne MsC 132.27.

*March 2011* N. W. BAWCUTT

# INTRODUCTION

## Description of the Manuscript

Osborne MsC 132.27 is one document in the 'Osborne Collection' of British manuscripts and rare books purchased in 1972 by the University of Calgary, in Alberta Canada, from the British antiquarian Edgar Osborne. The University of Calgary collection includes 'ballads, letters, play, parliamentary documents, speeches, petitions and applications for letters patent'.[1] In 2004, an interdisciplinary research group was formed to examine and transcribe the untitled, anonymous play and to determine its provenance.

The manuscript is written on paper in folio, with folios numbered 1–26 in the same light brown ink and hand employed for the text of the play. A preliminary page, unnumbered and blank on the verso side, lists 'The Persons of the play' in the same ink and hand (Plate 1). A blank folio of the same paper serves as a paper cover. On the front cover Osborne has written:

Watnall Hall Sale
1947
No title, No effort
made to trace authorship.
Handwriting c Mid or later
17th Century
Edgar Osborne.
More likely 18th Century.

The manuscript is 31.1 cm long and 20 cm wide; all pages are within 2 mm of these dimensions. Stab marks in the left margins of every page indicate it was once bound into one gathering, although the binding is almost fully deteriorated. Dark residue along the once bound edge suggests that it may have been glued to a more substantial cover. The pages are worn and frayed though no text appears to have been lost on the recto leaves.

There are two watermark designs in the manuscript. One is a one-handled pot with the letters 'C | A B' and the other an anchor with the letters 'I' and 'G' suspended from the crossbar. The anchor design is found on folios 21–6 and on the unnumbered page that contains the list of characters; the pot design is found on all other leaves. Both watermarks are found near the centre of the leaf. The scribe employs a mixed secretary hand, with the list of characters, speech prefixes, and stage directions written in italic. Stage directions are either centered on the page or to the right of the dialogue and most often are contained by a half-bracket or enclosed in a box. While it is generally a clean and tidy manuscript, there is evidence of both eye skips,

[1] From the University of Calgary Special Collections description: <http://specialcollections.ucalgary.ca/manuscript-collections/international-archival-holdings-/edgar-osborne>.

suggesting that the scribe is copying, and composition, suggesting authorial intervention. The verso leaf of each folio contains a catchword for the next recto leaf.

Osborne MsC 132.27 is a comedy in five acts set in a country shire. Key characters are Justice of the Peace Thrifty, his daughter Constance, her suitor Christopher Spruce, Spruce's mother Mistress Mumble, his friend Wild, Thrifty's clerk Peter Parchment, Peter's wife Jennet, the King of the Shepherds and his numerous companions. This manuscript is a revised version of the same play, also untitled and anonymous, preserved in a miscellany at Arbury Hall, Warwickshire.[2] The miscellany contains four plays, three untitled. In the 1980s Trevor Howard-Hill published articles on these dramas and provided names for the three unnamed plays, calling the play with Justice Thrifty *The Humorous Magistrate.*[3] In one of these articles, 'Another Warwickshire Playwright: John Newdigate of Arbury', he argues that John Newdigate III (1600–42) is the author of all four plays.

An idiosyncrasy of the Osborne scribe links him or her to plays in the Arbury Hall miscellany (though not to the Arbury version of *The Humorous Magistrate*): the use of the musical repeat sign ://: to direct the repetition of phrases. Siobhan Keenan notes in her Introduction to the Malone Society edition of *The Emperor's Favourite* (another play in the Arbury miscellany) that the same combination of virgules and colons appears in that manuscript, as well as in the Arbury miscellany plays *Ghismonda and Guiscardo* (f. 82) and *The Twice Chang'd Friar* (f. 33). Paul Faber identifies this sign as signaling 'textual repetition'; he finds its similar use beside the lyrics in William Child's *The First Set of Psalms of III Voyces* (1639).[4] It appears that the number of repeat signs signals the number of times the line is meant to be repeated. Keenan notes that in *The Emperors Favourite* the sign appears four times at line 3803 after the words 'Iustice Iustice'. The sign appears only once, however, after each of the following phrases in the Osborne version of *The Humorous Magistrate:* 'Breakeing wind eases an old woman extremelye'; 'yes, the | more is my harme'; and 'I haue bene much deafer since the | last training' (Plate 2).[5]

While the Osborne manuscript might be called a 'fair copy' of the author(s)' work, the Arbury manuscript displays rigorous revision. In 'Near Neighbours:

[2] See the Malone Society edition of the Arbury Hall version of the play, edited by Margaret Jane Kidnie (Manchester, 2012).

[3] See 'Boccaccio, *Ghismonda*, and its Foul Papers, *Glausamond*', *Renaissance Papers* (1980), 19–28, and 'Another Warwickshire Playwright: John Newdigate of Arbury', *Renaissance Papers* (1988), 51–62. The play in the Arbury miscellany provided with a name by the scribe is *The Twice Chang'd Friar*.

[4] Paul L. Faber, 'Crosswords: Textual and Thematic Similarities in *The Humorous Magistrate* and *The Emperor's Favourite*'. Unpublished conference paper read at the meeting of the Canadian Society for Renaissance Studies (Congress of the Humanities and Social Sciences) University of British Columbia, Vancouver, 31 May 2008.

[5] The sign appears in Osborne MsC 132.27 after lines 283, 284 and 285. Henceforth, lines from the Arbury and the Osborne versions of the play will appear in parenthesis in the body of the introduction.

Another Early Seventeenth-Century Manuscript of *The Humorous Magistrate*', Margaret Jane Kidnie concludes that 'Osborne's obvious partial dependency on the Arbury manuscript, combined with its substantial structural and verbal changes and refinements, strongly indicates that at least one stage of revision, perhaps more, lies between these two extant manuscripts.'[6] The differences between the two versions of the play are examined in more detail later in this introduction.

## Provenance

Scholars agree that the documents in the Arbury miscellany, assembled and bound in the early eighteenth century, have always been associated with the Newdigate family, who acquired Arbury Hall in 1586. The provenance of the Osborne manuscript, however, has not yet been satisfactorily determined. Edgar Osborne was the county librarian for Derbyshire from 1923 to 1954 and an active collector of and dealer in books and manuscripts for most of his life (1890–1978). His most notable contribution is his collection of some 2,000 rare examples of children's literature in manuscript and print, which he donated to the Toronto Public Library in 1949. It was through this link to Canada that the sale to Calgary was negotiated in the early 1970s, when the university was young and establishing its library.

Watnall Hall, the residence of the Rolleston family from the late sixteenth century, was located near Nottingham, but was demolished in 1962. We began our research on the provenance of the Osborne manuscript by looking for evidence of a sale at Watnall Hall in 1947. We found no such evidence, but a catalogue is held by the Local Studies Library in Nottingham for an auction of the contents of the Hall, managed by Walker, Walton & Hanson, in 1954. There is no listing for a manuscript play among the items from the Hall library listed in the auction catalogue. A study of Osborne's papers held by the Derbyshire Record Office reveals, however, that he had frequent dealings with Watnall Hall. He seems to have attended the 1954 auction, as evidenced by one title in the auction catalogue which Osborne lists under the title 'Jan 56 Inventory of Valuable books at the Spinney' (his Derbyshire home): 'George Shelvocke's *A Voyage round the world by way of the great south sea* | London, 1726 | Purchased Watnall Hall Sale'.[7] Also in the Spinney inventory is a book held in the Calgary collection: Lucio Oradini's 1550 edition of *Due Lezzioni*. On the inside of the hardbound cover, Osborne notes 'Woolescroft 1941'. His faithfully kept wartime diaries record trips to Woolescroft and to Watnall Hall, where the last Rolleston heir, Maud, was disposing of her books.

[6] Margaret Jane Kidnie, 'Near Neighbours: Another Early Seventeenth-Century Manuscript of *The Humorous Magistrate*', *English Manuscript Studies 1100–1700*, 13 (2007), 187–211 (p. 201).

[7] Derbyshire Records Office D5063/18, 'Jan 56 Inventory of Valuable books at the Spinney', Edgar Osborne.

After his retirement as county librarian, Osborne was sought out as a knowledgeable antiquarian by owners of large estates. In 1955 he was appointed librarian at Hatfield House and, fortuitously, he acted in the same capacity through the 1950s and 1960s at Arbury Hall.[8] We find Osborne's hand and indeed a signed comment among the manuscripts still held at Arbury Hall and speculate that he may have organized them for microfilm reproduction. The miscellany that contains the Arbury version of *The Humorous Magistrate* is among these manuscripts and on a blank leaf preceding the plays in the miscellany, we find the following note in Osborne's hand: 'Manuscript Plays of considerable interest E O a414'. The information about Osborne's close association with Arbury Hall, along with records that speak to Osborne's vast amount of buying, selling, cataloguing and brokering over nearly fifty years, of course raises the suspicion that the Osborne manuscript of *The Humorous Magistrate* may have actually been acquired at Arbury Hall and not Watnall Hall and that Osborne may have added his annotation to the Calgary manuscript sometime after its acquisition and misremembered its provenance. When we next looked closely at the extant inventories of the Arbury Library, we found that none contains a record of this manuscript play in folio (though most include mention of the miscellany). There are, however, many entries in the 1855 and 1888 inventories for 'miscellaneous' tracts and plays in both print and manuscript.

Another avenue of research to the same end has been the investigation of potential associations between the seventeenth-century Newdigate and Rolleston families. Watnall Hall and Arbury Hall were only forty miles apart and as M. J. Kidnie demonstrates in 'Near Neighbours', both Arbury Hall and Watnall Hall were very close to estates owned and inhabited by the Willoughby family. The estate of Middleton, located next door to Arbury Hall, was the Willoughby family seat for five hundred years. In the 1580s, the Willoughby family began construction of Wollaton Hall in Nottinghamshire, on family property situated next door to Watnall Hall. Kidnie locates evidence linking the Willoughbys and Rollestons in 1592 by way of the sale of land by Sir Francis Willoughby that would add to the marriage settlement for Edward Ballard and Valentyne Rolleston made between the couple's fathers, Edward Ballard and Lancelot Rolleston. We find a link between the next generation of the Willoughby family and John Newdigate III in the latter's Commonplace Book, held at the Bodleian Library.[9] In Newdigate's hand, we find a poem titled 'Mr. Clifton to my Cousin An Willoughby'.[10] The assignation 'cousin' suggests a neighbourly closeness.

[8] Research Assistant Kirsten Inglis examined a file of correspondence at Hatfield House between Osborne, Lord Salisbury and the library assistants. There was no reference to manuscript drama.

[9] Bodleian Library, Oxford, MS Eng. Poet e.112, ff. 1–73.

[10] 'An Willoughby' was likely the daughter of Sir Henry Willoughby of the Risley, Derbyshire, branch of the family.

We have identified links between the family of William Cavendish, Duke of Newcastle, and the Rollestons of Watnall and the Newdigates of Arbury as well. John Rolleston, the long-time literary scribe for William and later Margaret Cavendish, was related to the Rollestons of Watnall. Among the correspondence and papers 'of Moseley of Carburton and Rolleston of Watnall-Chaworth, co. Notts; 1619–1740', at the British Library, there are two letters from John Rolleston to his cousin William Rolleston. One concerns outstanding debts to the family and is written from the Cavendish estate at Welbeck Abbey; in the other, catalogued as 'Note on the pedigree of Rolleston', John Rolleston names 'Oure house of Wattnall Chaworth' the family seat.[11]

Further, among the Newdigate papers at the Warwickshire County Record Office is the only extant copy of an extensive list of the fish and fowl served at the Duke of Newcastle's festivities given for King Charles I and Queen Henrietta Maria in 1634. The list is titled 'A note of the Earle of Newcastles fowle at the feast he made the King at Bolsover, 1634'. Item CR 136 B 2453 was located by research team member Kirsten Inglis, who observes that the detail given suggests that the document is an eye-witness account. Of course for students of drama, the description of the feast provides a context for Ben Jonson's masque *Love's Welcome to Bolsover*, commissioned for the occasion, and which incorporates the feast into the dramaturgy of the performance.[12] Were the Newdigates and the Rollestons of Watnall Hall in attendance at this grand occasion? It would have been a long journey for the Newdigates from Arbury Hall at some seventy miles, although Watnall Hall was not twenty miles from Bolsover.

Our expanding team of collaborators has investigated the archives of Osborne as well as the Newdigates, the Rollestons and their associates in eight archives in the United Kingdom and three in the United States. We approached our archival work with many questions, but have always kept in mind the outstanding question of the provenance of the University of Calgary version of *The Humorous Magistrate*. No concrete evidence confirming or refuting the provenance attributed by Osborne has emerged. Nevertheless, the Osborne manuscript appears to be a fair copy that could have been prepared for circulation among the Midland gentry.

## Dating

In 'Near Neighbours', M. J. Kidnie approaches the dating problem and the author question by making a comparative study of the hands and watermarks represented in the Osborne manuscript, the dramatic manuscripts

[11] BL Additional MS 34,769, items 32 and 39.

[12] Our thanks to Dr Julie Sanders, who shared her recollection of seeing a reproduction of the 'menu' from the Newdigate archive in the Bolsover Castle guidebook, written by Dr Lucy Worsley.

found in the Arbury miscellany and in other documents in the Newdigate archive at the WCRO. She concludes that the hands found in the Arbury and Osborne manuscripts date to around the second quarter of the seventeenth century and are similar in their use of a secretary script through which is scattered italic forms. She finds a poem in the miscellany dated 1637 that shares a watermark found in the Arbury version of *The Humorous Magistrate* and concludes that 'the combination of hands and watermarks found in the Arbury miscellany and Osborne copy serves to establish an outer limit for the composition of *The Humorous Magistrate* to near or shortly after 1637'.[13] In Mary Polito and Jean-Sébastien Windle's '"You see the times are dangerous": the Political and Theatrical Situation of *The Humorous Magistrate*', Windle's research into topical reference in the play also supports a date of composition in the 1630s.[14] He argues that the play alludes to two documents issued by Charles I aimed particularly at governing Justices of the Peace (and about which Thrifty complains in the play): *The Book of Orders,* issued in 1631, and 'A Proclamation Commanding the Gentry to Keepe Their Residence at Their Mansions in the Countrey and Forbidding Them to Make Their Habitations in London, and Places Adjoyning', issued in January 1632.[15] In '"You see the times are dangerous"', Polito describes a further and highly significant topical allusion, first noted by Jacqueline Jenkins, which is found only in the Osborne version and leads to the determination of a *terminus a quo* for the Osborne manuscript's production. The allusion is to an order issued by King Charles and Archbishop Laud in May 1640: 'Known colloquially as "the Etc. Oath", the order was Canon 6 of "seventeen cannons" directed at all governors, secular and clerical, in the realm. Each was to "swear that I do approve the doctrine, and discipline, or government established in the Church of England ... by archbishops, bishops, deans, and archdeacons, &c." The "&c." in the oath was instantly suspect.'[16] Many, if not most, refused to sign the oath and the project was abandoned in November of the same year. The allusion is inserted into the Osborne version of the play on folio 3a as Peter the clerk and scribe converses with Thrifty (Plate 3):

*Thrif*: ....yo$^{r}$
*Neotericall* gentleman is yo$^{r}$ onelye accepted thing, which
I will proue a *simile*.
*Pet*. The comparison will hold S$^{r}$, both in the new fashiond titles
*et id genus alia quae nunc perscribero. Etc*
*Thrif*: O w$^{th}$out an *&c* good Peter, by all meanes w$^{th}$out an *&c*.

13 Kidnie, p. 198.

14 Mary Polito and Jean-Sébastien Windle, '"You see the times are dangerous": the Political and Theatrical Situation of *The Humorous Magistrate*', *Early Theatre*, 12 (2009), 93–118.

15 James F. Larkin (ed.), *Stuart Royal Proclamations. Volume II, Royal Proclamations of King Charles I, 1625–1646* (Oxford, 1983), pp. 350–3.

16 Polito and Windle, p. 109.

*Pet.* Why S$^{r}$, *&c* is sense, els learned men would not sweare to't.
*Thrif*: Sweare to't? what sweare to an &c? (210–17)

Further evidence that goes to dating the play provided in the *Early Theatre* article links *The Humorous Magistrate* to Richard Brome's *A Jovial Crew* (1641–2).[17] Both plays utilize a plot involving old patriarchs, travelling vagabonds and models for an alternative 'commonwealth'. In both, the alternative communities welcome musicians into their company and in the Osborne version of *The Humorous Magistrate* and *A Jovial Crew* characters remark upon the recent conviction of musicians for singing libelous songs. The most direct links, however, involve characterization and actual snippets of dialogue. Brome's Justice Clack and Thrifty share a catch-phrase in 'I told you before', and both brag about their judicial practice, which involves sentencing the accused before hearing the case. It appears that one of these authors saw a manuscript or performance of the other's work before or while composing the works above, though we have not determined the direction of influence. Nevertheless, the links suggest again that *The Humorous Magistrate* is of late Caroline provenance.

## Complex Revision

Eric Rasmussen observes that '[e]very extant dramatic manuscript from the period shows signs of revision'.[18] Rasmussen distinguishes revisions that may be categorized as simple addition and subtraction from 'complex revision' that involves 'the addition of sizable new scenes and more complex intricate revisions that often involved hundreds of minor changes'.[19] We suggest that what we find in the Osborne manuscript is just such a 'complex revision' that derives from the Arbury manuscript and/or subsequent versions. That is, the revisions are more extensive than simply cutting or adding and involve such elements as the rethinking of everything from plot development to individual poetic lines. In the Osborne we find more explicit stage directions, the substitution of one geographical reference for another and many other small, and sometimes puzzling, alterations.

Material cut from the Arbury, or its derivative, in the making of the Osborne version includes a prologue and epilogue, a Scottish or perhaps northern character named Jony and the whole theme of horse-racing and gambling. Material is substantially rearranged in the Osborne so that the romances between Thrifty and the widow Mumble and between Wild and Spruce's sister Sophia are established much earlier in the play. There are dozens of small revisions, some of which seem to move from specific references to the more general. For example, there is an overt reference to Hamlet

[17] For evidence that Brome's play was performed in spring 1642, see Matthew Steggle's 'Redating *A Jovial Crew*', *Review of English Studies*, 53 (2002), 365–72.

[18] Eric Rasmussen, 'The Revision of Scripts', in *A New History of Early English Drama*, ed. John D. Cox and David Scott Kastan (New York, 1997), pp. 441–60 (p. 441).

[19] Rasmussen, p. 453.

in the Arbury manuscript. Spruce (sometimes 'Spruse' in the Arbury) offers a long soliloquy on his thwarted love for Thrifty's daughter Constance and Wild accuses him of acting like a 'randing player' (Arbury 221)[20] and gesturing as if he 'were acting Hamlet' (Arbury 235). In the Osborne, 'acting Hamlet' is replaced with 'acting to yo$^{r}$ glass' (163). See Plate 4 in this edition and for comparison Plate 6 in the Malone Society Arbury edition of *The Humorous Magistrate*. In the Osborne, an addition to the same dialogue suggests that Spruce should be costumed like the inky-cloaked Hamlet. Wild declares that he himself:

... will not goe in black,
Except in lent to be a formall courtier,
Or specious mourner at a funerall. (145–7)

A similarly puzzling revision occurs in allusions to London locations. In the Arbury, Wild chides Spruce about being in love: 'Is't possible the singing of *Cupids* arrowes | should be heard at [an ordnary] m$^{ris}$ yardlyes' (228–9);[21] in the Osborne the line reads 'is't possible the singing of chast *Cupids* arrows | should be heard at *Peccadillye*' (157–8). While this reference to a London district replaces one to a specific eating establishment, another reference to a London locale, intriguingly 'the Phenix Tauern' (339), appears only in the Arbury.

While the Arbury version is more than a thousand lines longer than the Osborne, the Osborne provides additions and substantial rewriting for the purpose of expanding the satire of Thrifty, most often by giving him more to say. With the excision of the Epilogue in Osborne, for example, Thrifty is given both the final speech as well as a much extended one on f. 25a, the penultimate folio (see Plate 5). The revisions reveal what can only be called tinkering as well. For example, in the Arbury we find Spruce complaining 'when a reall torm$^{t}$ | Contendsw$^{th}$in the heart must burst or yeeld' (2229–30); in the Osborne the lines read 'when a reall torment | Contends w$^{th}$in, the heart must yeeld, or breake' (1403–4). The author substitutes a word, adds a caesura, slightly refining the poetic line that bears Spruce's complaint. Readers may wish to compare Plate 10 in the Arbury edition with Plate 6 in this edition for another example of the playwright's tinkering.

The Osborne version also seems to represent some decisions made in the light of performance or at least a staged reading of the play. For example, the satire of the officious judge that is built into Thrifty's catchphrase 'as I told you before' occurs in both versions; yet there are far fewer 'as I told you befores' in the Osborne than the Arbury as if the author has apprehended, in some way, the point where the joke gets stale. The stage direc-

[20] Line 221 in the Malone Society edition of the Arbury version of the play; 152 in this edition.

[21] The scribe first wrote 'm$^{ris}$ yardlyes', then deleted it and inserted 'an ordnary'. He then changed his mind, deleted 'an ordnary', and reinserted m$^{ris}$ yardlyes' as an interlineation.

tions are more extensive in the Osborne as well. For example, there is a new instruction for the actor who would play Mistress Mumble. She is not only to sing her line 'Now Lawyer I defy thee doe thy worst' (Arbury 1154), in the Osborne, '*she wipes her mouth sings the next line | to the tune of K. Arthur*' (764–5). Kidnie concurs with Howard-Hill that the plays represented in Arbury A414 'point to a playwright who seems to have written with the prospect of production'.[22] The discovery of the Osborne manuscript only strengthens this case and may indeed imply an active dramaturgy informing the revision process.

## Paleography and the Question of Authorship

Our research has been wide ranging, our eyes open for authorial candidates. Circumstantially, John Newdigate remained a viable candidate, his interest in drama revealed in many ways in the Newdigate archive: the vast number of seventeenth-century dramas in translation as well as playbooks published in the period listed in the nineteenth-century inventories; dramas in manuscript at the WCRO such as those penned by men associated with Oxford when brothers John and Richard Newdigate were studying there. Included in the Arbury Hall miscellany, though not adjacent to the four plays noted above, is a manuscript of *The Mountebank's Masque* titled 'The Style of Henry the Second Prince of Grayers Inne Anno Dm. 1617'.[23] We also find in the account books that John attended plays at various London venues. An interest in contemporary politics, with a particular focus on George Villiers, the Duke of Buckingham, is evident in the eclectic collection of seventeenth-century manuscripts in the Newdigate archive, which contains parliamentary speeches, ballad libels, a Ship Money Bill and other treatises and pamphlets representing the political debates from the 1620s to the 1640s. Yet, no empirical proof about authorship had emerged until the paleographical study by Boyda Johnstone and Kirsten Inglis was undertaken.

Johnstone and Inglis first located late autograph documents by John Newdigate and began a systematic comparison with the Osborne hand, made possible by the ability to isolate and juxtapose letter and word formations in digitized documents. M. J. Kidnie observed that:

> There is, in fact, a good match for the Osborne hand to be found in the Arbury miscellany, but not in the drama. A one-page poem that precedes the plays, entitled 'To a Poet whose m$^{ris}$ was painted' (the uncorrected title reads 'Vpon a painted gentlewoman') and dated August, 1637, exhibits the same distinctive scribal characteristics one finds in the Osborne manuscript.[24]

[22] Kidnie, pp. 204–5.

[23] A production of the masque, the Arbury Hall version reports, 'was presented in the banquetting house at whitehall before the King and the Prince on Thursday night in Shrove weeke the 19 of Febr A$^{o}$ 1617' (A.414 f. 6b). For a brief account of this anonymous entertainment see G. E. Bentley, *The Jacobean and Caroline Stage*, 7 vols. (Oxford, 1941–68), V, 1376–8. Bentley was not aware of the existence of this manuscript.

[24] Kidnie, p. 198.

The 'hand charts' created by Johnstone and Inglis from the Osborne manuscript, the poem and a two page letter from Newdigate dated 1637 provide convincing evidence that John Newdigate was at least the scribe of the Osborne version of the drama. They have gone much further in their investigation, however, including an examination and comparison of the hands represented in all the extant documents attributed to John Newdigate III as well as the hands of his brother and their associates. The convincing conclusion of Johnstone and Inglis is that Newdigate not only penned all the plays in the Arbury miscellany, but that he also authored them.[25]

## Conventions Employed in this Edition

The following conventions have been observed in this diplomatic edition. Square brackets enclose deleted material. Angle brackets enclose obscure or illegible text; dots within the angle brackets indicate illegible characters (⟨..⟩). Interlined words are lowered into the text and noted in the textual notes; carets are not printed in the text, but are indicated in the notes. Line numbering has been supplied by the editors and is continuous for the text of the play and includes headings and stage directions (if they occur on a separate line). The position of words, lines, speech-prefixes, headings and stage directions is reproduced as exactly as is possible, though slight misalignments are overlooked. Stage directions, speech prefixes and, rarely, some words of the text are larger in the manuscript than the rest of the play; in the edition, however, differences in letter-size have been regularized throughout.

The text of the play is written in secretary script within which is found occasional italic forms; secretary script in this edition appears in roman typeface, and the scattered italic letter forms are not noted. Speech-headings and stage directions are written throughout in italic script, as are some proper names and phrases in the body of the text; these are all represented in this edition by the use of italic. Secretary ampersand is represented by '&', while the italic ampersand is represented by '*&*' (see lines 215–23).

The original spellings, punctuation and abbreviations in the manuscript have been retained in the edition. Tildes in the manuscript usually appear as a large curved arc and are represented in the edition by a small curved line above the relevant letter. Scribal use of 'per' and 'pro' ligatures has been retained in the edition (see, for example, lines 86, 230, etc., and line 475). Superscript letters are represented in superscript form. Long 's' has been regularized, as has terminal 's', since there is no obvious or consistent orthographic significance to it. Original capitalization has also been retained, although in some cases determining whether letters are capitalized or not in initial line position, for instance, or in the abbreviation for 'Mr' or 'Mris',

[25] See Inglis and Johnstone, '"The pen lookes to be canoniz'd": John Newdigate III, Author and Scribe', *Early Theatre*, 14 (Dec. 2011), 27–61. This is a special issue on the 'Osborne Project' findings, co-edited by Amy Scott and Mary Polito.

has been a matter of editorial judgement; in the manuscript, majuscule and miniscule forms of some letters, for instance 'm' and 'y', are often very difficult to distinguish. Throughout the manuscript, exclamation marks and question marks are nearly always indicated by the same symbol, thus distinction between the two forms of punctuation in the edition has also been a matter of editorial judgement. Alterations of and corrections to individual letter forms and words are recorded in the notes; the original letter or word is not indicated in the edition but is provided in the note when it is still distinguishable. As well, marks in the margin are recorded in the notes but are not indicated in the edition.

The pages in the Plates have been reproduced at approximately 56 per cent of full size.

## Acknowledgements

The editors would like to thank the following institutions and funding agencies for assistance with the edition: The University of Calgary and the Special Collections at MacKimmie Library, The Social Sciences and Humanities Research Council of Canada, and the Warwickshire County Record Office. In addition, we would like to thank Lord Daventry for permission to cite from MS A.414. We are also very grateful to Apollonia Steele (of Special Collections, University of Calgary) for her unflagging enthusiasm and individual support for our investigation of the Osborne manuscript play and Susan Bennett, our co-investigator on the SSHRC funded research project. We thank Malone Society editor Nigel Bawcutt for his guidance and keen eye as we prepared this edition. Thanks are due as well to the several University of Calgary graduate students who contributed in various ways to the research represented in the introduction and in the creation of this edition, especially Boyda Johnstone, Kirsten Inglis, Paul Faber, John Siddons, Owen Stockden, Jean-Sébastien Windle, and Amy Scott.

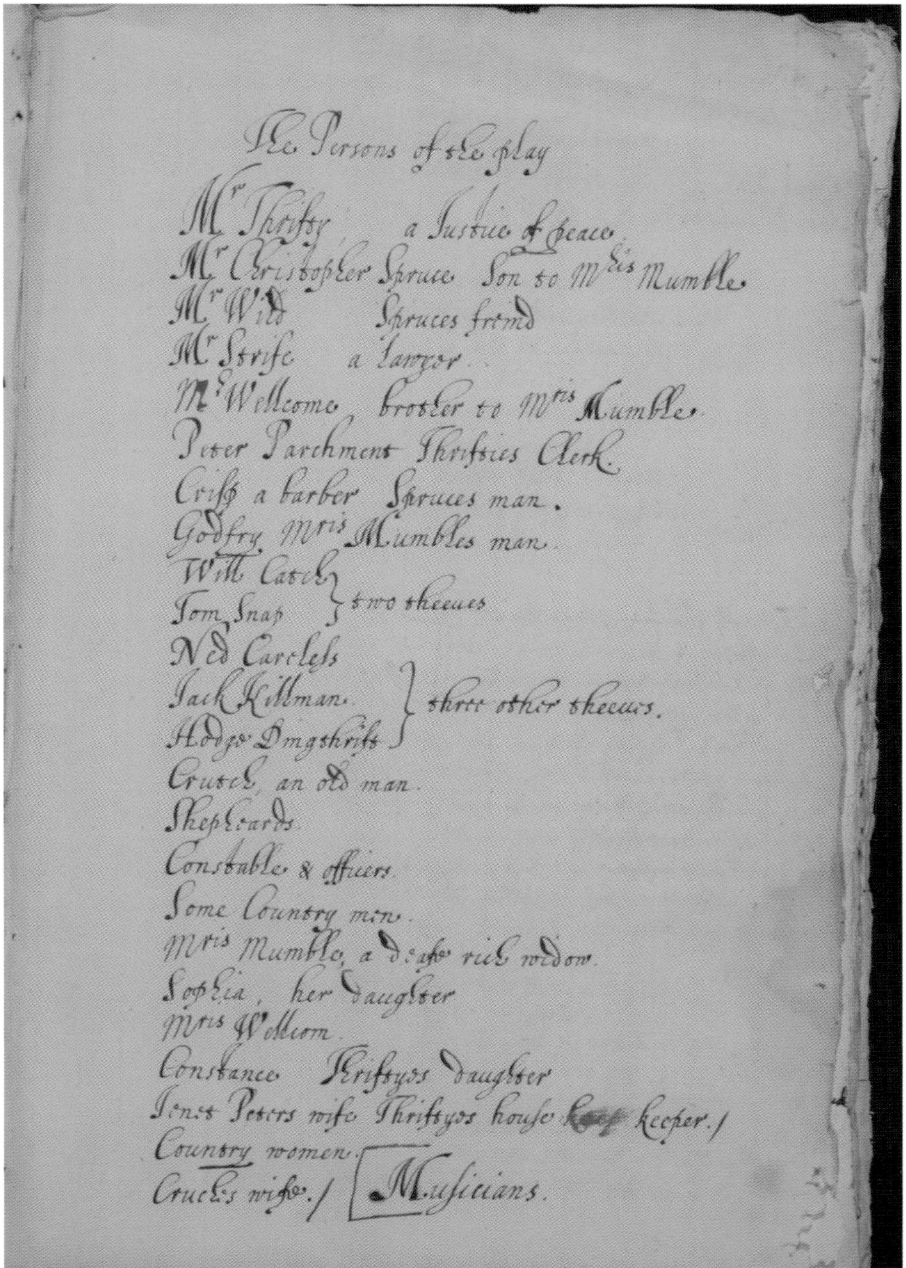

The Persons of the play

Mr Thrifty a Justice of peace
Mr Christopher Spruce Son to Mtris Mumble
Mr Wild Spruces friend
Mr Strife a Lawyer
Mr Wellcome brother to Mtris Mumble
Peter Parchment Thrifties Clerk
Crisp a barber Spruces man.
Godfry Mtris Mumbles man
Will Catch }
Tom Snap } two theeves
Ned Carelesse }
Jack Killman } three other theeves.
Hodge Dingthrift }
Crutch an old man.
Shepheards.
Constable & officers.
Some Country men.
Mtris Mumble, a deafe rich widow.
Sophia, her daughter
Mtris Wellcom.
Constance Thriftyes daughter
Jone Peters wife Thriftyes house ~~keep~~ keeper./
Country women.
Crutch's wife./ Musicians.

Plate 1: (Dramatis personae) unnumbered first page

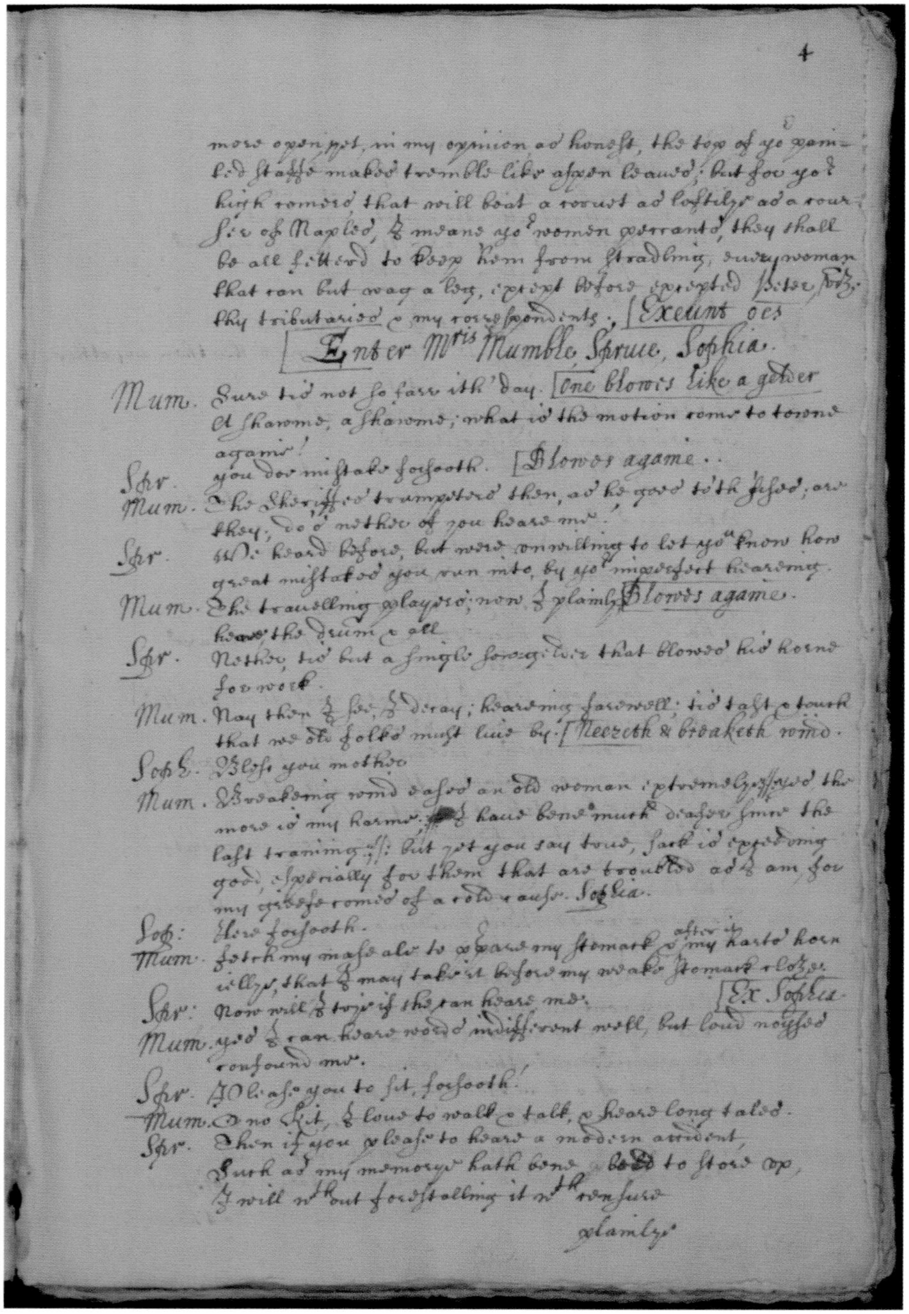

PLATE 2: FOL. 4A (FOR AN INSTANCE OF ://:)

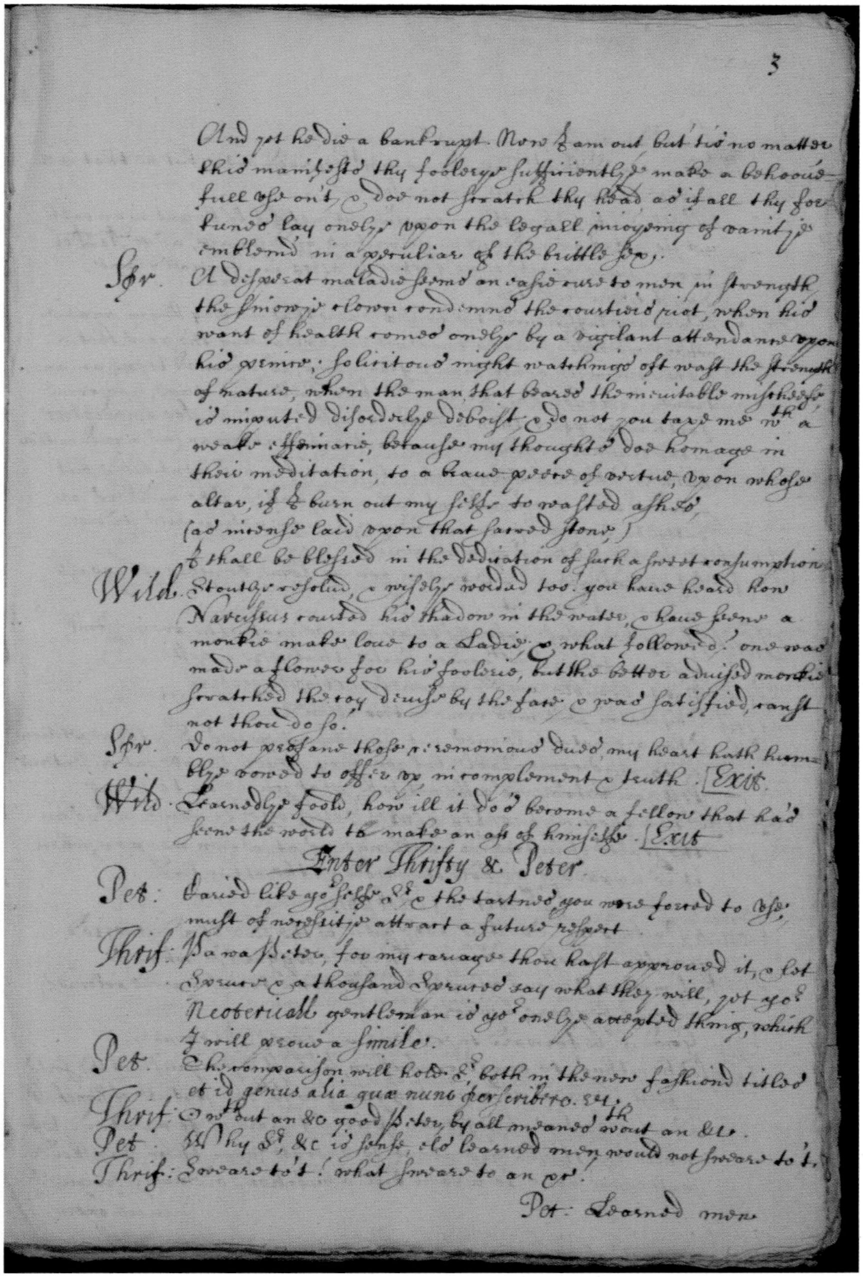

3

And yet he die a bankrupt. Now I am out, but tis no matter
this manifests thy foolerye sufficiently, & make a blushfull
full use on't, & doe not scratch thy head as if all thy for
tunes lay onelye upon the legall moyeing of vanitye
embleme in a peculiar of the brittle sex.

Spr. A desperat maladie seems an easie cure to men in strength
the sincere clown condemns the courtiers diet, when his
want of health comes onelye by a vigilant attendance upon
his service; solicitous night watchings oft wast the strength
of nature, when the man that beares the inevitable mischeife
is reputed disorderlye deboist, & do not you taxe me wth a
weake effeminacie, because my thoughts doe homage in
their meditation, to a beautye peere of vertue, upon whose
altar, if I burn out my selfe to wasted ashes
(as incense laid upon that sacred stone)
I shall be blessed in the dedication of such a sweet consumption

Wild. Stoutlye resolved, & wiselye worded too. you have heard how
Narcissus courted his shadow in the water, & have seene a
monkie make love to a Ladie, & what followed? one was
made a flower for his foolerie, but the better advised monkie
scratched the coy deuise by the face & was satisfied, canst
not thou do so.

Spr. do not profane those ceremonious dues, my heart hath humblye vowed to offer up in complement & truth. [Exit

Wild. Friendlye foole, how ill it does become a fellow that has
seene the world to make an ass of himselfe. [Exit

Enter Thrifty & Peter

Pet: carried like yor selfe Sr & the tartness you were forced to use,
must of necessitye attract a future respect

Thrif: Ha wa Peter, for my cariage thou hast approved it, & let
Spruce & a thousand Spruces say what they will, yet yor
Neotericall gentleman is yor onelye accepted thing, which
I will prove a simile.

Pet. The comparison will hold Sr, both in the new fashiond titles
et id genus alia quæ nunc perscribere &c.

Thrif. O wth out an &c good Peter, by all meanes wth out an &c.

Pet. Why Sr, &c is sense, old learned men would not sweare to't.

Thrif: Sweare to't! what sweare to an &c!

Pet: Learned men

Plate 3: Fol. 3a (for Etc. oath)

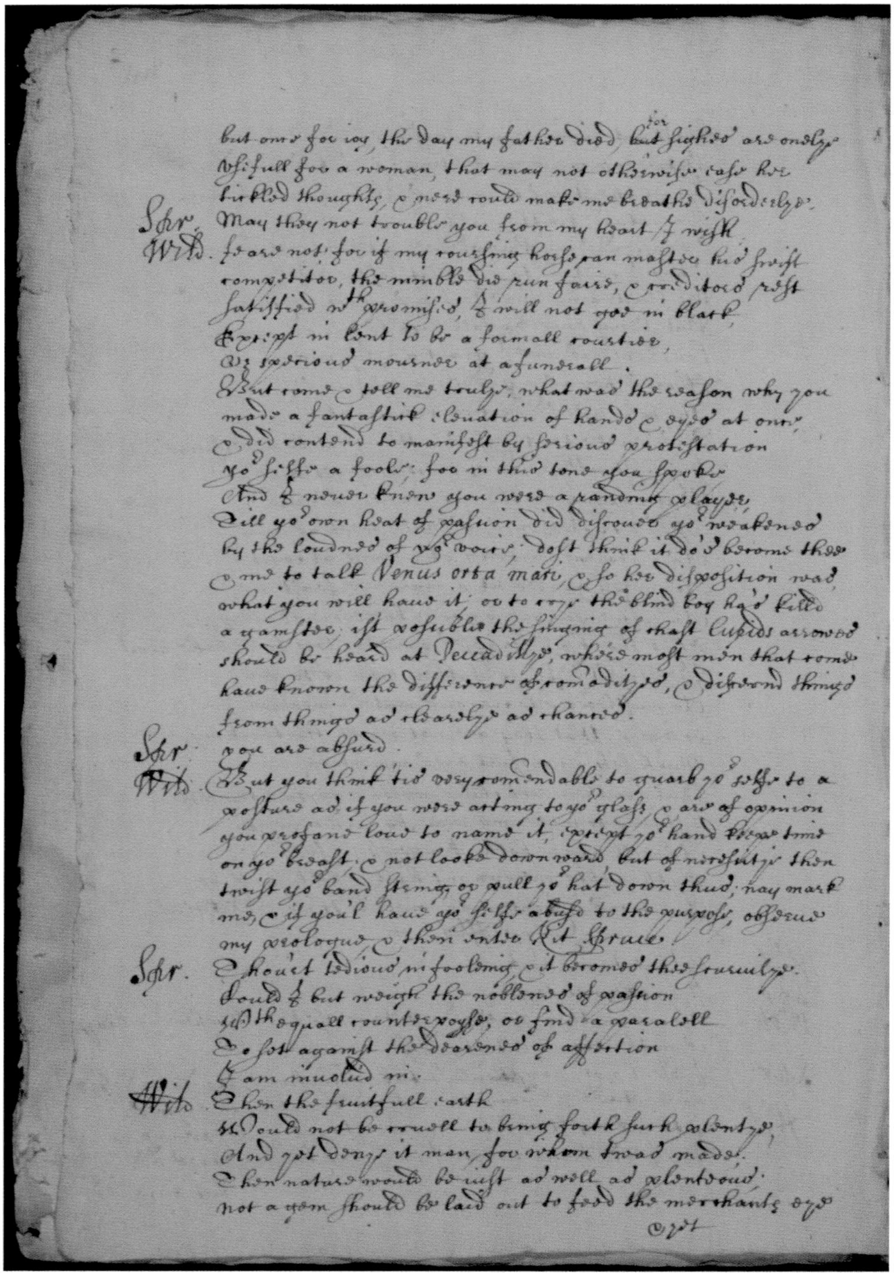
but once for ioy, the day my father died, but for sighes are onely
usefull for a woman, that may not otherwise ease her
tickled thoughts, & mine could make me breathe disorderlye.
Shr. May they not trouble you from my heart I wish
Wild. feare not, for if my couzsins horse ran master his first
competitor, the nimble did run faire, & creditors rest
satisfied wth promised, I will not goe in black
Except in Lent to be a formall courtier,
Or a serious mourner at a funerall.
But come & tell me truelye, what was the reason why you
made a fantastick elevation of hands & eyes at once,
& did contend to manifest by serious protestation
yor selfe a foole; for in this tone you spoke
And I never knew you were a randing player,
Till yor own heat of passion did discover yor weakenes
by the loudnes of yor voice, dost think it do's become thee
& me to talk Venus orta mari, & so her disposition was
what you will have it, or to cry the blind boy ha's killd
a gamster, ist possible the singing of chast Cupids arrows
should be heard at Peccadillye, where most men that come
have known the difference of commodityes, & discerne things
from things as clearelye as chance.
Shr. you are absurd.
Wild. But you think tis very commendable to quarb yor selfe to a
posture as if you were acting to yor glass, & are of opinion
you profane loud to name it, except yor hand be at time
on yor breast, & not look downward but of necessitye then
twist yor band strings, or pull yor hat down thus; nay mark
me, & if you'l have yor selfe abusd to the purpose, observe
my prologue, & then enter Kit Spruce.
Shr. Thou'rt tedious in fooling, & it becomes thee scurvilye.
Could I but weigh the noblenes of passion
With equall counterpoyse, or find a paralell
To set against the deareness of affection
I am involud in.
Wild. Then the fruitfull earth
Would not be cruell to bring forth such plentye,
And yet deny it man for whom twas made.
Then nature would be iust as well as plenteous:
not a gem should be laid out to feed the merchants eyes
Yet

PLATE 4: FOL. 2B (FOR COMPARISON WITH ARBURY PLATE 6, REVISION OF 'HAMLET' TO 'RANDING PLAYER')

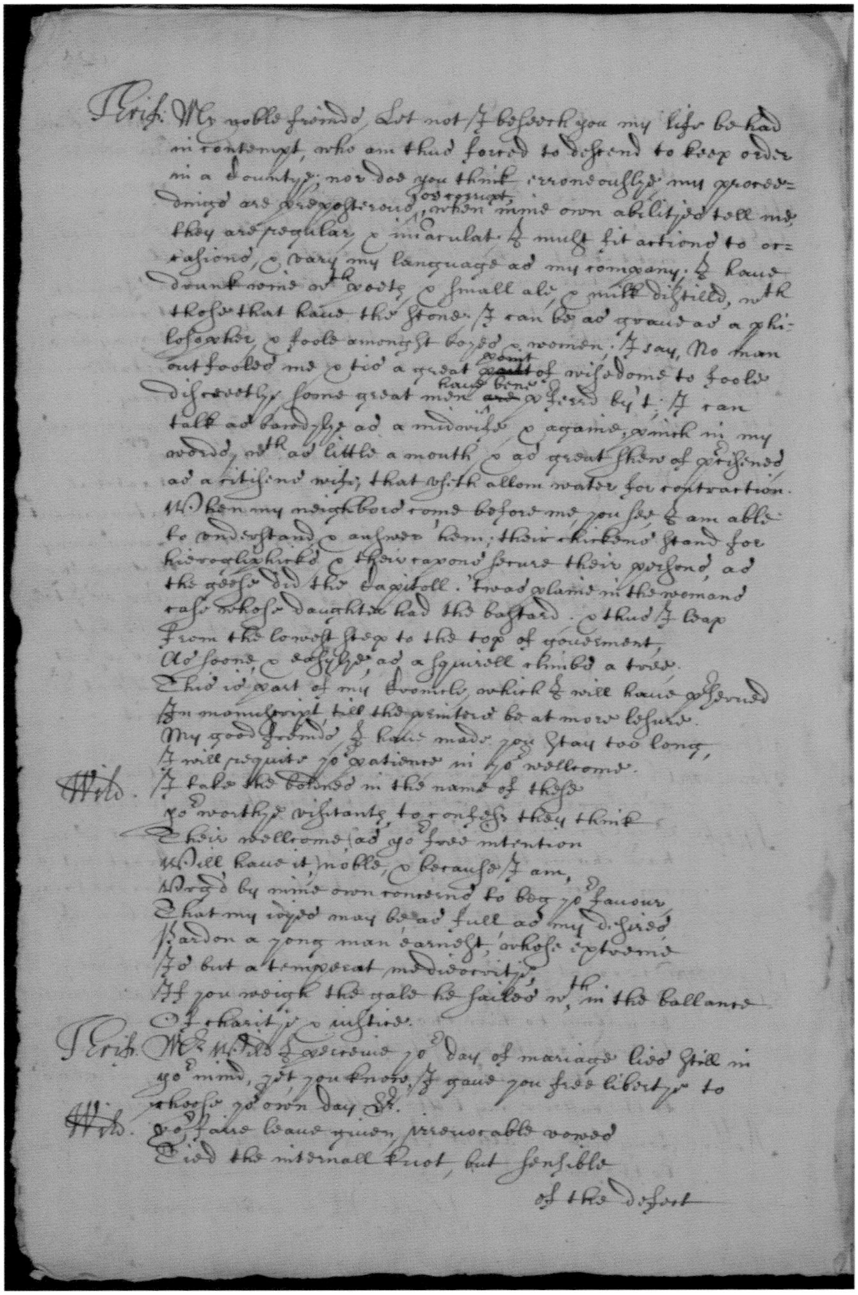
Thrif. My noble friends, Let not I beseech you my life be had
in contempt, who am thus forced to descend to keep order
in a country; nor doe you think erroneously my proceed=
ings are preposterous, when mine own abilityes tell me,
they are regular & irregular. I must fit actions to oc=
casions, & vary my language as my company. I have
drunk come ... ... & small ale, & milk distilled, with
those that have the stone. I can be as grave as a phi=
losopher, & foole amongst boyes & women. I say, No man
out fooled me, & tis a great point of wisdome to foole
discreetly, some great men have been advised by't. I can
talk as bawdyly as a midwife & againe, pinch in my
words, with as little a mouth & as great shew of precisenes
as a citizens wife, that sith allom water for contraction.
When my neighbors come before me you see I am able
to understand & answer them; their chickens stand for
hieroglyphicks & their capons secure their persons, as
the geese did the Capitoll. 'twas plaine in the womans
case whose daughter had the bastard. & thus I leap
from the lowest step to the top of government,
As soone & easily, as a squirrell climbs a tree.
This is part of my chronicle, which I will have preserved
In manuscript till the printers be at more leisure.
My good friends I have made you stay too long,
I will requite yo<sup></sup>r patience in yo<sup></sup>r wellcome.
Wild. I take the boldnes in the name of these
yo<sup></sup>r worthy visitants, to confesse they think
Their wellcome (as yo<sup></sup>r free intention
Will have it) noble, & because I am,
Urged by mine own concerns to beg yo<sup></sup>r favour
That my joyes may be as full as my desires
Pardon a yong man earnest, whose extreame
Is but a temperat mediocrity;
If you weigh the zeale he failes with in the ballance
Of charity & iustice.
Thrif. Mr Wilde Experience yo<sup></sup>r day of mariage lies still in
yo<sup></sup>r mind, yet you know, I gave you free liberty to
choose yo<sup></sup>r own day &c.
Wild. Yo<sup></sup>r faire leave given, honorable vowes
Tied the internall knot, but sensible
of the defect

PLATE 5: FOL. 25B (FOR EXPANSION OF THRIFTY'S SPEECH AND ROLE)

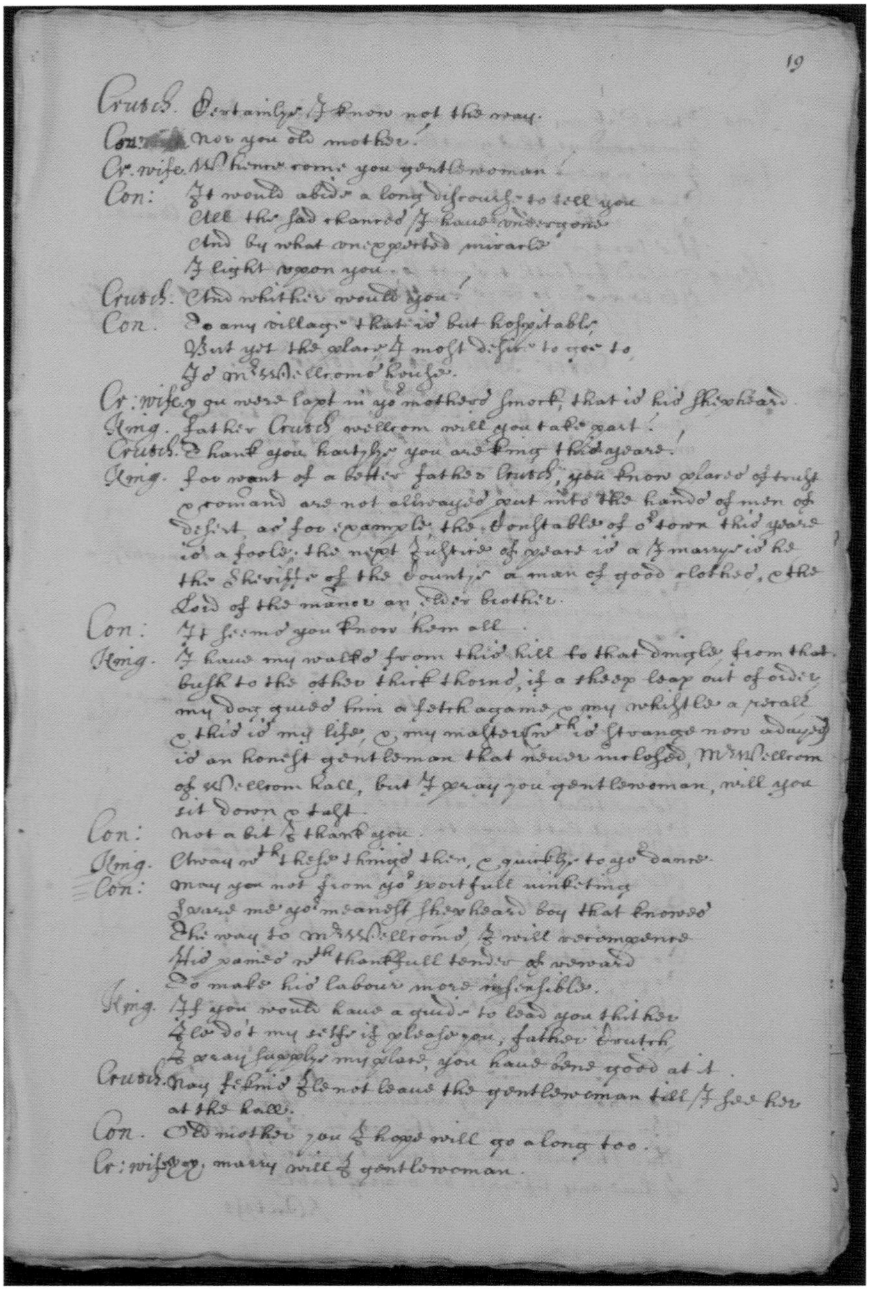

19

Crutch. Certainlye I know not the way.
Con: Nor you old mother!
Cr. wife. Whence come you gentlewoman!
Con: It would aske a long discourse to tell you
All the sad chances I have undergone
And by what unexpected miracle
I light upon you.
Crutch. And whither would you!
Con. To any village that is but hospitable;
But yet the place I most desire to goe to
Is Mr Welcomes house.
Cr: wife. You were kept in yor mothers smock, that is his shepheard.
King. Father Crutch welcome will you take part!
Crutch. I thank you heartilye you are king this yeare!
King. For want of a better father Crutch, you know places of trust & comand are not allwayes put into the hands of men of desert, as for example the Constable of or town this yeare is a foole, the next Justice of peace is a [illegible] marrye is he the Sheriffe of the Countie a man of good clothes, & the Lord of the manor an elder brother.
Con: It seems you know them all.
King. I have my walks from this hill to that dingle from that bush to the other thick thorne, if a sheep leap out of order my dog guides him a fetch againe, & my whistle a recall & this is my life, & my master [illegible] is strange now adayes is an honest gentleman that never [illegible], Mr Welcome of Welcome hall, but I pray you gentlewoman, will you sit down & tast.
Con: not a bit I thank you.
King. Away wth these things then, & quickly to yor dance.
Con: may you not from yor sportfull meetings
Spare me yor meanest shepheard boy that knowes
The way to Mr Welcomes I will recompence
His paines wth thankfull tender of reward
To make his labour more insensible.
King. If you would have a guide to lead you thither
Ile doe't my selfe if please you, father Crutch
I pray supplye my place, you have bene good at it.
Crutch. Nay [illegible] Ile not leave the gentlewoman till I see her at the hall.
Con. Old mother you I hope will goe along too.
Cr: wife. Ay marry will I gentlewoman.

Plate 6: Fol. 19a (for comparison with Arbury Plate 10, a relatively stable scene, but with 'tinkering')

*The Persons of the play*

| | |
|---|---|
| *Mr Thrifty* | *a Iustice of peace* |
| *Mr Christopher Spruce* | *Son to Mris Mumble* |
| *Mr Wild* | *Spruces freind* |
| *Mr Strife* | *a lawyer* |
| *Mr Wellcome* | *brother to Mris Mumble* |
| *Peter Parchment* | *Thrifties Clerk.* |
| *Crisp a barber* | *Spruces man .* |
| *Godfry* | *Mris Mumbles man .* |
| *Will Catch* / *Tom Snap* | } *two theeues* |
| *Ned Careless* / *Iack Killman* / *Hodge Dingthrift* | } *three other theeues.* |
| *Crutch, an old man* | |
| *Shepheards .* | |
| *Constable & officers .* | |
| *Some Country men .* | |
| *Mris Mumble, a deafe rich widow .* | |
| *Sophia, her daughter* | |
| *Mris Wellcom .* | |
| *Constance* | *Thriftyes daughter* |
| *Ienet Peters wife* | *Thriftyes house [keep] keeper. /* |
| *Country women .* | |
| *Cruches wife . / [M]usicians .* | |

*Act . 1 .* [Fol. 1a]

*Enter Mr Thrifty & Mr Spruce.*

*Thrif*: Sr I desire you to forbeare pressing me further, till I haue better informd my selfe of some things I am yet vnsatisfied in.

*Spr*: If by a Zealous importunitye
I seeme imõdest, 'tis yor daughters worth
That makes me press thus earnestlye, & I
Am confident, you rather doe deferr

yo$^{r}$ oft implor'd assent to set an edge
On appetite, (although impossible
To be made more acute,) then cruelly
To denye my suit, & by a sad subuersion
Ruine me, & my fortunes

*Thrif*: M$^{r}$ Spruce,
I tell you againe, we men of parts & com̃and doe consider
much, we haue authoritye to consider, I, to consider, de=
termin & execute; now the three actions are to be
performed by parties iointlye or seuerally, as yo$^{r}$ consi=
deration is to be done by my selfe *per se,* or w$^{th}$ my
brother Iustices *cum alijs*; the determination onely by
the aduise consent & assent of my clerk Peter Parchment
& my selfe, (for you know euer a sufficient clerk lookes
in the statute book to see what his master may doe) & ex=
ecution by the Constable, bedle, hangman, or some such or=
dinary rascall, therefore I say, I will consider, good M$^{r}$
Spruce, I will consider.

*Spr*. S$^{r}$, doe but please to giue me free permission
To lay my seruice at yo$^{r}$ daughters feet
Till you shall think expedient by resolue
To answer me, or to appoint a day
When I may know yo$^{r}$ pleasure. *[Pulls out his Almanack & lookes vpon it*

*Thrif*: I canot S$^{r}$. for thus stands the appointment, Munday the
ouerseers account, Tuesday the Sessions, Wensday high
wayes, Thursday bridges, friday alehouses, & Saturday
bastard

bastard children; S$^{r}$ all my time is taken vp, & you must [Fol. 1b]
wait my leisure, or let yo$^{r}$ suit fall. Peter. Peter.
Is not this booke the true directer *Enter Peter*
of affaires?

*Pet*: As prouidence can designe, or pen write down, S$^{r}$.

*Thrif*: Then I will consider further; Peter knowes we euer
take time to consider

*Pet*. Euer S$^{r}$, you destroy the grauitie of iustice els, & make
yo$^{r}$ authoritie contemnd.

48 *Parchment*] *P* rewritten

*Thrif*: M$^{r}$ Spruce, I tell you you must be satisfied or authoritye
shall silence you. *Exit.*

*Pet*. There's a bob for you, M$^{r}$ Spruce, & so we leaue you
though my M$^{r}$ be not yet I am a clerk of the *quorum*

*Spr*. O stupiditye in the robes of iustice, thy *Ex. Peter*
clerks eccho, & the ale wifes patron, the beggars
torment, & the iailors freind; the whores persecuter,
yet thine own minds baud, thou seller of iustice, & buyer
of capons, w$^{th}$ the breach of thine oath, & betraying of
thine own vnderstanding, of less extent then thy
conscience, how miserablye plagued is my deare
*Constance*, to haue such a thing to her father, as canot
read English but in his clerks hand, nor euer
wrote suꝑscription, but to the Constable, or his deputye,
& that vpon cap paper;
Hath heauen vouchafd to bless the fruitfull earth
W$^{th}$ opulencie, & denied man licence
To make it vsefull, when his eager palat,
(Pincht w$^{th}$ extreme necessitye) begins
To faint for want of meat? hath plenteous nature
Descended to inlighten mans capacitye,
W$^{th}$ a peculiar singlenes of obiect,
Clearer in essence, & in opposition,
Then the app$^{r}$hensiue sense to w$^{ch.}$ it was
Accounted passiue,? & yet in strict reuenge
Of my vnworthye valueing that gem
Mine eyes had glimpse of, but their amazed pupills
Durst not
Durst not examine, interpos'd a cloud [FOL. 2a]
Betweene me, & my blessing; yes, tis yeelded,
I call the starrs to witnes, things goe wrong
In nature, for the sublim'd eminence
Transcends my knowledge, & let me not be punish't
That I contend to rise that loftye pitch,
My fluttering imperfections canot reach,
But being once vp, fall back to ground againe;

73 *you you*] second *you* interlined above caret 79 *persecuter,*] , below line under *r* 88 *vouchafd*] *sic*, scribe's normal spelling (cf. 956, 1236, etc.) 102 *blessing;*] question mark appears above semi-colon

*Constance* is pure,! grant a religious preist
Adore's her as a goddess, & performs
The holy rites deuotion can inuoke;
Tis smoke that rise's, & though it be a perfume
Inrich't w$^{th}$ prime extractions, yet it is
But vapour, or the excrement of gum̃
Offer'd to clearenes, w$^{ch}$ will meet as euen,
As a clownes morris at a mask at court,
Or cipress apples at a mariage feast.
And since you are so good, therefore, shall I,
That think yo$^{r}$ prayses, (farr too low to speake 'hem)
Be slighted by yo$^{r}$ father, who is to you,
As mustles are to curious waterd pearles,
So vglye, that they are not worth the touching,
Much less a carefull eyes inspection,
But for their rich childs worth; appeare thy selfe,
I scorne to make my way, by such a person
As will abuse both Emperess, & subiect,
My thoughts out run my hast, & both shall be
Ambitious in contention, onely to thee |*Exiturus*

*Enter Wild*

*Wild.* What to me *Kit*, ha!
*Spr*: I spoke not to you
*Wild.* To whom then prithee dost thou vse to talk when no bodye is in the roome but thy selfe?
*Spr.* I vse it not, nor would I take exceptions, should yo$^{u}$ desire in a retired priuacie to vent yo$^{r}$ troubleous sighes.
*Wild.* I thank my starrs, care neuer strook so deepe in me, for I did neuer weepe since I was three yeares old
but once
but once for ioy, the day my father died, [but] for sighes are onelye [Fol. 2b] vsefull for a woman, that may not otherwise ease her tickled thoughts, & nere could make me breathe disorderlye.
*Spr.* May they not trouble you from my heart I wish.
*Wild.* feare not; for if my coursing horse can master his swift competitor, the nimble die run faire, & creditors rest

111 *holy*] *h* altered from *l* 134 *would*] *w* altered from *sh* 139 *for sighes*] *for* interlined above deletion; caret below deletion

satisfied w$^{th}$ promises, I will not goe in black,
Except in lent to be a formall courtier,
Or specious mourner at a funerall.
But come & tell me trulye, what was the reason why you
made a fantastick eleuation of hands & eyes at once,
& did contend to manifest by serious protestation
yo$^{r}$ selfe a foole; for in this tone you spoke,
And I neuer knew you were a randing player,
Till yo$^{r}$ own heat of passion did discouer yo$^{r}$ weakenes
by the loudnes of yo$^{r}$ voice; dost think it do's become thee
& me to talk *Venus orta mari*, & so her disposition was,
what you will haue it; or to crye the blind boy ha's killd
a gamster; is't possible the singing of chast *Cupids* arrowes
should be heard at *Peccadillye*, where most men that come
haue known the difference of com̃odityes, & discernd things
from things as clearelye as chances.

*Spr*: you are absurd.

*Wild*. But you think 'tis very com̃endable to guarb yo$^{r}$ selfe to a
posture as if you were acting to yo$^{r}$ glass, & are of opinion
you profane loue to name it, except yo$^{r}$ hand keepe time
on yo$^{r}$ breast; & not looke downward, but of necessitye then
twist yo$^{r}$ band string, or pull yo$^{r}$ hat down thus; nay mark
me, & if you'l haue yo$^{r}$ selfe abusd to the purpose, obserue
my prologue, & then enter *Kit Spruce*.

*Spr*. Thou'rt tedious in fooleing, & it becomes thee scuruilye.
Could I but weigh the noblenes of passion
W$^{th}$ equall counterpoyse, or find a paralell
To set against the dearenes of affection
I am inuolu'd in.

*Wild*. Then the fruitfull earth
Would not be cruell to bring forth such plentye,
And yet denye it man, for whom twas made;
Then nature would be iust as well as plenteous;
Not a gem should be laid out to feed the merchants eye
& yet
And yet he die a bankrupt. Now I am out, but 'tis no matter, [Fol. 3a]
this manifests thy foolerye sufficientlye, make a behooue=

180 *matter,*] , below line under *r*

full vse on't, & doe not scratch thy head, as if all thy for=tunes lay onelye vpon the legall inioyeing of vanitye emblem'd in a peculiar of the brittle sex.

*Spr.* A desperat maladie seems an easie cure to men in strength, the sinowye clown condemns the courtiers riot, when his want of health comes onelye by a vigilant attendance vpon his prince; solicitous night watchings oft wast the strength of nature, when the man, that beares the ineuitable mischeefe, is imputed disorderlye deboist, & do not you taxe me w$^{th}$ a weake eff⟨en⟩inacie, because my thoughts doe homage in their meditation, to a braue peece of vertue, vpon whose altar, if I burn out my selfe to wasted ashes,
(as incense laid vpon that sacred stone,)
I shall be blessed in the dedication of such a sweet consumption

*Wild.* Stoutlye resolud, & wiselye worded too! you haue heard how *Narcissus* courted his shadow in the water, & haue seene a monkie make loue to a Ladie; & what followed,? one was made a flower for his foolerie, but the better aduised monkie scratched the coy deuise by the face, & was satisfied, canst not thou do so?

*Spr.* Do not profane those ceremonious dues, my heart hath hum=blye vowed to offer vp, in complement & truth. [*Exit.*

*Wild.* Learnedlye foold, how ill it do's become a fellow that ha's seene the world to make an ass of himselfe. [*Exit*

*Enter Thrifty & Peter.*

*Pet*: Caried like yo$^{r}$selfe S$^{r}$, & the tartnes, you were forced to vse, must of necessitye attract a future respect.

*Thrif*: Pa wa Peter, for my cariage thou hast approued it, & let Spruce & a thousand Spruces say what they will, yet yo$^{r}$ *Neotericall* gentleman is yo$^{r}$ onelye accepted thing, which I will proue a *simile*.

*Pet.* The comparison will hold S$^{r}$, both in the new fashiond titles *et id genus alia quae nunc perscribero. Etc*

*Thrif*: O w$^{th}$out an *&c* good Peter, by all meanes w$^{th}$out an *&c*.

*Pet.* Why S$^{r}$, *&c* is sense, els learned men would not sweare to't.

*Thrif*: Sweare to't? what sweare to an &c?

*Pet*: Learned men

191 *effeninacie*] *en* written together; minim error by scribe (too few minims for 'effeminacie')

205 *to*] *o* altered from *h*

*Pet.* Learned men I assure you, S$^{r}$. [Fol. 3b]

*Thrif*: Ile not meddle w$^{th}$ learning, nor w$^{th}$ learned men, but he that will sweare to an &c. shall sweare for me

*Pet.* Well S$^{r}$, but though you conclude it not fit to be put in an oath yet yo$^{r}$ &c is as needfull in yo$^{r}$ writing or discourse, as yo$^{r}$ *Ao Doi* vpon a signe poast, or yo$^{r}$ *fertur ad astra* in a funerall elegie.

*Thrif*: Sayst thou so Peter?

*Pet.* Vpon my sufficiencie tis true S$^{r}$; now that we may begin againe where we left, for you know we were cleareing the point that a new sprung vp gentleman & flourishing, is receaued before an an=tient & decayed one, yo$^{r}$ wor:$^{pp.}$ ha's this aduantage, you come forth more ꝑfect then a booke reuised, & are *multo emendatior* in the originall copie, when yo$^{r}$ antient gentleman, (as a good author hath it,) hath nothing more to shew for his gentilitye, but records, then most authenticall when rotten like medlers, or eaten to peeces by a reuerend worm in an antiquaries studie.

*Thrif.* O feeble builders of a piramid!

*Pet.* If you please S$^{r}$, Ile reckon you vp some knights oth'poast of antient descent.

*Thrif*: Hang 'hem base rascalls their names make the roome stink, foule my fingers w$^{th}$ comõn baile! that were a iest.

*Pet.* Not to trouble you S$^{r}$, but onely *exempli gratia.*

*Thrif*: Thy Latin sentences come in too often.

*Pet.* They are not whole ones, but significant peeces S$^{r}$, & the repetition of them is comẽndable, but you may neuer speake out a sentence, lest you betray yo$^{r}$ selfe not to be, what you desire to seeme.

*Thrif* Then thou & I *contra gentes Peter*, offer to weigh w$^{th}$ vs in the scales of iustice,? or challenge vs at o$^{r}$ own weapon, when it is apparant we hold the sword in the other hand?

*Enter a Constable.*

*Con.* Worthye m$^{r}$ Thriftye, take pitye of the side of a distressed parish, allmost ouer-run w$^{th}$ rogues beggars & whores.

*Thrif*: A most notorious plantation, like some transmarine colonies, rogues, beggars, & whores.

*Con.* Good S$^{r}$, be forward to releeue an oppressed corner.

*Thrif*: Then thus, to auoyd confusion, I must distinguish of the sorts & first there is yo$^{r}$ court beggar, for w$^{ch}$ the statute of *Winchest$^{r}$*

238 *make the*] illegible character interlined between *e* and *t*

is yet defectiue, howsoeuer officers timorous to app$^{r}$hend, lest while we should goe about to execute vpon them, they should pass vpon vs, & so a ram kill a butcher; ordinarye rogues

more open .

more open, yet, in my opinion, as honest, the top of yo$^{r}$ pain= [FOL. 4a]
ted staffe makes tremble like aspen leaues; but for yo$^{r}$ high comers, that will beat a coruet as loftilye as a cour=ser of Naples, I meane yo$^{r}$ women peccants, they shall be all fetterd to keep 'hem from stradling, euery woman that can but wag a leg, except before excepted Peter, *Viz.* thy tributaries & my correspondents. [*Exeunt oes*

[*Enter M$^{ris}$ Mumble, Spruce, Sophia.*

*Mum.* Sure tis not so farr ith'day. [*One blowes like a gelder* A shawme, a shawme; what is the motion come to towne againe?

*Spr.* You doe mistake forsooth. [*Blowes againe.*

*Mum.* The Sheriffes trumpeters then, as he goes to'th 'sises; are they; do's nether of you heare me?

*Spr.* We heard before, but were vnwilling to let yo$^{u}$ know how great mistakes you run into, by yo$^{r}$ imperfect heareing.

*Mum.* The trauelling players; now I plainly [*Blowes againe.* heare, the drum & all.

*Spr.* Nether, tis but a single sow=gelder that blowes his horne for work.

*Mum.* Nay then I see, I decay; heareing farewell; tis tast & touch that we old folks must liue by. [*Neezeth & breaketh wind.*

*Soph.* Bless you mother

*Mum.* Breakeing wind eases an old woman extremelye://:yes, the more is my harme;://: I haue bene much deafer since the last training ::://: but yet you say true, sack is exceeding good, especially for them that are troubled as I am, for my greefe comes of a cold cause. *Sophia.*

*Sop*: Here forsooth.

*Mum.* fetch my mase ale to p$^{r}$pare my stomack & after it my harts horn iellye, that I may take it before my weake stomack cloze.

*Spr*: Now will I trye if she can heare me. [*Ex Sophia*

284, 285 *://:*] see introduction, p. viii  284 *://:*] written above deletion  *bene*] open circle above line after *bene*  289 *after it*] interlined above caret

*Mum.* yes I can heare words indifferent well, but loud noyses
confound me.
*Spr.* Please you to sit, forsooth!
*Mum.* O no Kit, I loue to walk & talk, & heare long tales.
*Spr.* Then if you please to heare a modern accident,
Such as my memorye hath bene [please] bold to store vp,
I will w$^{th}$out forestalling it w$^{th}$ censure
plainlye
Plainlye deliuer each occurrence to you. [FOL. 4b]
True iests in my opinion are the best,
Though they be bitter, & serious relations
Weakelye attract attention, not com̃and it,
When those that heare 'hem, think 'hem fabulous.
*Mum.* I loue to heare a tale, a part whereof
I know to be, or not to be my selfe.
*Spr* When you haue heard it, I am confident
you'l say tis so, & so, & tell the meaneing, better then any other.
*Mum.* It may be so, begin good Kit, begin.
*Spr.* As the earth hath varietie of obiects,
So men of various dispositions
Looke w$^{th}$ dislike, or approbation on 'hem.
Some affect sports, some seriousnes, some loue
The warrs, some peace & rest; some are content
To looke on fixed obiects; & others satisfie
The more ignoble senses, & [all] most end
In sad repentance; & lest that tediousnes
Should seeme to haue the mastrie, yea perhaps
Get it against o$^{r}$ will, & we, being men,
Should shew our selues, less rationall then beasts,
Not to com̃and or beare o$^{r}$ passions,
We giue our ioyes & sorrowes leaue to mixe.
Els 'twere, incomparablye, the brauest art,
Im̃ediatlye to catch at im̃ortalitye,
W$^{th}$out respectiue helps, or those conducements
That ease vs in the way, & nere attend
The tedious hand of death, w$^{ch}$ comes too slowlye
To men p$^{r}$pared. But since mortalitye

297 *bold*] written over deleted *please* 316 *most*] interlined over deletion; caret below deletion

Is iudg'd (w$^{th}$out recall,) to casuall failing,
To certaine interruption, & denyeall
Of long continuance,) in the very word
That signifies mortalitye; a man (not denied
The priuiledges others doe inioye)
And) next of all in the degree of blood
To you (deare mother,) valueing chastitie
Before impure misscalld delights, not reall
To those that vse 'hem, but exemplarye & vsefull
To them
To them that hate those beastlye practises, [Fol. 5a]
Hath not w$^{th}$ ouer valueing selfe loue
Hugg'd, but imployed, in a manlye way,
Affection, not lustfull appetite.
The day was geniall, when his first designe
Tooke life, iudiciall Astrologie
Approued the season, the propitious signe
Stood where he would haue wisht, & euery circumstance
Mou'd w$^{th}$ so faire a probabilitye,
Success was yeelding; but then happines
Had come too soone; perfect felicitye
Hath not so quick a generation,
Because the setled perpetuitye
Is of a longer residence. But then
His grasping thoughts extended soft imbraces,
And catcht the interposed rubb, w$^{ch}$ staid
Him from a sweet fruition.

*Mum.* I bless my heareing, & haue not a long time heard so perfectlye, but yet I vnderstand you not.

*Spr.* Then mother, receaue w$^{th}$ patience that w$^{ch}$ yo$^{r}$ child will tell you, since it is onely to make his fortunes, & yo$^{r}$ comfort.

*Mum.* Now I begin to be more deafe againe.

*Spr.* If I be troublesome, I will cease.

*Mum* No Kit, no.

*Spr.* But I shall raise my voice, & speake distinctlye.
By yo$^{r}$ faire permission [gaue me] I had leaue to make mine own free choice, I in despight of censure setled my mind; the

357 *yet*] *y* altered from *p* 364 *By*] added in left margin *I had*] interlined over deletion; caret below deletion

miserable carle, & father to the admirable virgin mainlye
excepted at the p$^{r}$sent maintenance you yearelye giue me,
& my disabilitye to make my wife a iointure, because the
land is yo$^{rs}$ for life; I durst not p$^{r}$sume to tell him I could
doe more, nor dare I yet, vntill you please to giue me
leaue to doe it.

*Mum.* O Kit now, I am deafer then at first

*Spr.* Then Ile speake louder.

*Mum.* No as thou louest me, for so I may ꝑhaps, greeueing
my troubled sense, be made vncapable of euer heareing
more.

*Spr.* If I perplexe you

Think you

Think you were young yo$^{r}$ selfe, think you were once [FOL. 5b]
As I am now onely the sex excepted,
And when I haue w$^{th}$ miserable extasie
Opend my heart in serious expression,
Ether releeue or ruine me, 'tis you
I liue to serue, & you must suffer if
I doe miscarye; doe but heare me out.
And I shall liue or die at yo$^{r}$ dispose.

*Mum.* I canot heare, I haue heard while I can, I was thick of heareing
before, but now I am deafe as an adder, I, & you haue made me so.

*Spr*: Ile take the boldnes to express my mind in writing, if my
words be so offensiue

*Mum.* I heare you not, I tell you once againe

*Spr*: Be not so wedded to yo$^{r}$ own conceit
As see me suffer, when a small proportion
Of what you haue, would make me swell w$^{th}$ plentie,
And thank my starrs, & you; if you desire
To haue the Lady named, for whose indearement
I doe thus humblye craue yo$^{r}$ charitye,
Tis the desert of *Constance* makes me press you,
Whom exception canot touch.

*Mum.* The wench is a good crout I fault her not, but if I giue thee
now, what wilt thou haue when I die.

369 *him*] interlined above caret 372 *am*] *m* altered from *n* 398 *Constance*] *e* rewritten

*Spr*: I am glad yo$^{r}$ heareing is recouered, I will but vse one other argument.

*Mum.* No on thy mothers word, I am deafe still, very deafe, exceeding deafe, passing deafe, extraordinary deafe, deafe, deafe, deafe.,

*Spr*: Then let me haue yo$^{r}$ licence to renounce my natiue soyle, & leave the place you gaue me my first being in, if such hard= heartednes liue in a mother to inforce me to so violent a course.

*Mum.* I loue thee Kit, O do not so my boy.

*Spr.* Why now you heare againe.

*Mum.* Very little.

*Spr.* Nay then haue at you, what if I in a rage should goe hang my selfe, & leaue a paper in my pocket, that Christopher Spruce hangd himselfe, because his mother would not make his wife a iointure, were not *M$^{ris}$ Mumble* guiltye think you?

*Mum.* Ill words in a boyes mouth, ill words in a boyes mouth; here take all my keyes, & riffle the iron chest to the very bottom the writings lie all there; pull down the houses, & then sell the bricks, cut down the trees because they shade the grass; then sell the land hang it it is but dirt, & of the monye thy wife may haue her thirds; or keep the land, & make it all in iointure, but no more words of hanging thy selfe, good Kit.

*Spr*: you'l take

[Fol. 6a]

*Spr*: You'l take away the cause, & then the effect
Canot succeed, Liberall & kind
Should liue ioint tenants in a parents mind *Exeunt.*

*Fin: Act .1.*

*Act .2.*

*Enter Thrifty, Constance, Peter. Ienet./*

*Thrif*: And as I told you girle, giue no answer of yo$^{r}$ selfe, but if I be out of the way, call Ienet to councell, & so proceed.

*Con*: S$^{r}$, I shall in obedience to you
Obserue yo$^{r}$ strict com̃ands, dutye binds,
And I shall yeeld, my care shall manifest
My dutye, & if both can inable me
To execute yo$^{r}$ plesure, no iniunction,
That comes from you, shall relish of dislike;
Though it seeme harsh to other app$^{r}$hensions.

*Thrif*: My good girle still, & as I told you *Iennet*, when yo$^{r}$ husband & I are abroad about the com̃on wealth affaires, let Constance sit at the tables end, but you keepe the key of the sack, for wine is [ill]

ill for girles, it breeds heat in their faces, & then they lay on black patches, w$^{ch}$ they say is all the fashion, but as I told you, me thinks it is very scuruie.

*Ienet* For that forsooth let yo$^{r}$ worp$^{s}$: mind be at quiet, clarified whey is excellent, all this time of the yeare, & though I say it before her face, my yong m$^{ris.}$ is very tidye, & passing tractable.

*Thrif*: The better still my good girle.

*Ienet.* Yes, Ile ensure yo$^{r}$ wor:$^{pp}$ for when her musick master was teaching her oth'lute, she would ⟨.⟩ know of me whether she did sit strait or no, & would not suffer him to turn vp her minikin, till she askt me whether I thought it would abide stretching.

*Thrif*: Good again, good againe, wonderfull good, vpon my worp:$^{full}$ word wonderfull good.

*Ienet.* No indeed forsooth; she will not willinglye haue a pin pinned about her, but I must be at the thrusting of it in, nor a knot tied, but I must giue my censure, whether it ioyne close or lye of a lump, & so be like to offend in the weareing.

*Thrif*: yet not w$^{th}$standing *Ienet*, if m$^{r}$ Spruce or any other picture of gallantrie chance to come, & protest like a gentleman; respect him worshipfullye, for I find by my selfe, 'tis not euery mans part to do gentleman like; & though I bought my arms of the herald & paid for 'hem too, yet sometimes I discouer my selfe to be a very clowne, therefore if m$^{r}$ Spruce come & protest like a gentleman, vse him as a gentleman thou Ienet in authoritye.

*Pet*: S$^{r}$ as yo$^{r}$ wor:$^{pp}$ makes bold w$^{th}$ me in things you vnderstand not, so I pray giue me leaue to ask you a question, what is it to protest like a gentleman.

*Thrif:* O thou

*Thrif*: O thou illiterd excrement of authoritye, not know that it is as essentiall to a gentleman to protest, as for thy maister to call a Constable Sirrah, attend & Ile instruct thee. [Fol. 6b]
To protest like a gentleman is to forsweare a mans selfe, but that can onelye be tryed by examinacõn of the thing, & so not proper for thy p$^{r}$sent instruction; but to protest like a gentleman, in breefe, is to protest in short, to ꝓtest at length, is to be done in more words, & to protest like

445 *all this time of the yeare,*] interlined above caret 452 *good againe,*] interlined above caret 475 ꝓ*test*] ꝓ altered from *p*

a gentleman, is to protest like a gentleman, dost not
vnderstand man?

*Pet.* But how S$^{r}$, I beseech you explaine yo$^{r}$ selfe.

*Thrif.* O how patient is Iustice, & how we men in office are
forc'd to beare w$^{th}$ the vulgar.

*Pet:* Trulye S$^{r}$, I vnderstand you not.

*Thrif.* No? why to protest like a gentleman is to protest like
a gentleman, & that is enough.

*Ien:* Enough of conscience, husband.

*Thrif:* O Ienet how do's thy capacitye exceed thy husbands! in
altitude & profunditye, in depth & compass, iust as my
dagger do's thy pen knife, Peter. *One knocks*
Strangers, strangers, you three tender
yo$^{r}$ fealtlye, that who beholds here the gouerment of a
republique, may, if he obserue, not go away vninstructed.

*Enter Spruce & Crisp.*

*Constance Pet: Ien: cursie to Thriftye a distance off*

*Spr.* Dick Crisp, do's the powder come neare the colour of my
haire?

*Crisp.* Yes S$^{r}$ tis a perfect ciuet powder, three pound an ounce.

*Spr:* Do the, curles of my perriwig turne gracefullye?

*Crisp.* As the Lords you desire to imitate, & me thinks yo$^{r}$
colour is farr more complete. *Crisp. stands off.*

*Spr:* W$^{th}$ yo$^{r}$ good fauour S$^{r}$.

*Thrif:* M$^{r}$ Spruce, good M$^{r}$ Spruce, you'r well amett S$^{r}$,
you'r well amett. M$^{r}$ Spruce I was a litte busye in
giueing rudiments to my familye.

*Spr.* Please you to haue it so S$^{r}$, I shall w$^{th}$draw.

*Thrif:* Good M$^{r}$ Spruce, the words of old men may doe you good
by way of p$^{r}$cept, & their cariage may instruct you [doe you good] by way
of example, as I told you before, therefore attend & be
edifyed, w$^{th}$ all my heart, good M$^{r}$ Spruce.

*Spr:* I shall S$^{r}$

*Spruce drawes neare to Constance; & talks w$^{th}$
her priuately.* [FOL. 7a]

*Spr.* I shall S$^{r}$.

*Thrif:* And as I told you Peter, write yo$^{r}$ examinacõns in a full hand.

499 *is*] *s* altered from *f* 502 *litte*] *sic*, scribal error for 'little' 506 *instruct you*] interlined above caret

*Pet.* Yes an't please you S$^{r}$.

*Thrif*: That as I told you, the clerk oth'sises associat may not curse you for scribling.

*Pet.* yes S$^{r}$.

*Thrif*: But as I told you may plainlye read the name of the examinat.

*Pet.* I dare warrant yo$^{r}$ wor:$^{pp}$ Ile write the cheefe words as taken before yo$^{r}$ wor$^{p}$:$^{p}$ & the like, in text letters.

*Thrif*: O absurd, very absurd, as I told you before; hast thou not my old clark Take=all's p$^{r}$sidents?

*Pet.* yes S$^{r}$, & his buckram bag, w$^{ch}$ a gentleman well studied in heraldrye councelled me to weare, as a pristin relique of an=tiquitye, because of the holes.

*Thrif*: Prosecute those p$^{r}$sidents, & follow the aduise of that buckram bag. And you Ienet euer before meales, bring me a cup of sack & a tost.

*Ien.* I forsooth.

*Thrif*: That as I told you before, by the expulsion of the wind I may [my Stomack being] make roome for my meat, that my stomack, being of small capacitye, may receaue nutriment w$^{th}$out disturbance.

*Ien.* I haue forsooth moreouer made you a diet ale, that taken in the morning, will giue you ease, w$^{th}$ out offence of any com=panye you come in, all the long day after; & yo$^{r}$ wor:$^{ps}$ box is neuer w$^{th}$out losinges of mine own makeing, I think you haue it now about you.

*Thrif*: Admirable good, my Ienet I protest, thou art most vsefull to me as I am a man in authoritye, but no more of that now.

*Ien*: O good S$^{r}$.

*Thrif*: Come, come obserue yo$^{r}$ charge, & follow yo$^{r}$ instructions; & good M$^{r}$ Spruce, doe not you think it a dishonour to be instructed amongst the rest; though as yet, yo$^{r}$ slight obseruation makes me suspect you doe not value what I say; or els my words are so deepe, you canot vnderstand [.]'hem.

*Spr.* If for a silent admiration
Of yo$^{r}$ words serious grauitye I seeme
Worthye of censure, rep$^{r}$hend yo$^{r}$ selfe
That so mistake a contemplation

517 *Pet. yes S$^{r}$.*] interlined    530 *I may*] interlined above deletion    536 *box*] interlined above caret

Setled in serueing you; or if you think
My obseruation

My obseruation was not so attentiue [FOL. 7b]
As yo$^{r}$ discourse expected; pardon me,
Here stands a beautie tied me to obserueance,
In satisfaction of whose least com̃and,
My life shall be powrd out a sacrifice
Before her shrine, & the expireing sufferer
Merit by dyeing, which sad solemnitye
Will honour her, create him happines,
And add to both.

*Thrif*: Ly da, you studied this S$^{r}$, did you not?

*Spr.* I could not speake till this saint gaue me vtterance,
But now I can declame eternallye
Vpon so braue a theme.

*Thrif*: Againe! satisfie an old man w$^{th}$out putting him to shew the extremitye of power in examination, did you not pen that speech, con it, & then deliuer it?

*Spr.* No S$^{r}$, I need not studie, pen or con,
Whilest this faire Ladye's by, the onely Muse
I doe inuoke, & whose strong influence
Inspires me more then all the other Nine.

*Thrif*: Then Peter, as I told you before, Iustice is an ass, & authoritye a dull fellow, & I see there's no offering at wit but in a womans companye. I will haue no more consultation w$^{th}$ dull *Bodinus de Republica*, but euer hereafter, get a hansom wench into my studie, to make my fancie work.

*Spr.* And yet you'l still be cruell; you see yo$^{r}$ daughter giues me my thoughts, my words, & tis an argument why you will haue a womans companye, at yo$^{r}$ more serious howres & graue retirement, then good S$^{r}$ do not remain inexorable, but after thus long giue me a word of comfort.

*Thrif*: M$^{r}$ Spruce both you & I conclude that women inspire & [&] gouern & we find by experience, that men doe daylye suffer, the Em=pero$^{r}$, & the bore, the philosopher, & the foole, some for accom̃odation, others because they know not how to help it; & as I com̃itt all matters of iustice to my clerk, so I doe

584 *[&] gouern &*] interlined above caret

the affaires of my estate, & matching my daughter to his wife that wholsome drie nurse M$^{ris}$ Ienet, that *remedium* that stands by you; 'tis true I assure you as I told you before, good M$^{r}$ Spruce.

*Spr*. S$^{r}$ if my

*Spr*: S$^{r}$, if my short liued memorye deceiue me not, you neuer told me so before, though you be pleased to say you did. [FOL. 8a]

*Thrif*: As I told you before S$^{r}$, is my word, I am affected to the phrase, S$^{r}$, & fault me not, if I lace my discourse w$^{th}$ as I told you, or as I told you before,; for men in my place haue their words by themselues, & I thought good to make choice of as I told you, before any other sentence S$^{r}$, therefore vnder=stand as I told you, & be satisfied as I told you before.

*Pet*: I beseech you S$^{r}$, vse my wife & my yong M$^{ris}$ |*Ex Thriftye* well, while my M$^{r}$ sleeps, I must dispatch some countrye busines. |*Ex. Peter./*

*Spr*. It is my honour farr aboue ambition
To be the seruant of this Ladies will.

*Con*. Curb'd by a fathers charge, I doe forbeare
T'express my selfe so freelye as I would;
My vndiscouerd will is confident
My patience shall be crownd, till then I may
But please my selfe w$^{th}$ thinking what an action
Must not giue life to yet.

*Spr*. I had not relisht ioy, so sensiblye,
If opposition had not made it pleaseing;
To want a meale, or two, instructs a man
How to set value on a liberall feast;
I fear'd & hop'd, I did assure my selfe,
Then sad despaire came sodainlye, & washt
That faire side off, w$^{ch}$ made a sweet appareance.
But now the Sun begins to be a victor,
faire weather comes w$^{th}$out the plowmans prayers,
Yet he's sole debter whom the benefit
Obligeth to be gratefull; I learne to make
An application, had you but smiled before,
My inward feare had blushd this second part

599 *S$^{r}$*] interlined above caret    605 rubbed mark in right hand margin

Had not bene reall; but the first born fruit
Is most times perfect, & the voluntarye stork,
That giues her young so freelye, is more noble
Then to demand that gift=bird back againe.
Pardon dread princess of my cogitations,
I doe compare in broken sentences
you & these
you & these much inferiours; yo$^{r}$ smiles [FOL. 8b]
Gaue me a courag'd boldnes; my humilitye
In thanks declares yo$^{r}$ bountye as you haue
Bene parent to my expectation,
Giue heat to warm it & to keepe it liueing.

*Con*: To flatter you, were to desire yo$^{r}$ ruin,
And to torment you w$^{th}$ a sad discouragement,
Were to offend against that virgin goodnes
I'm tender of, & confident you value highlye

*Spr.* May all my words,
Catch poyson in the aire, & thence returne
Infected vapours into the breast where they
Were first conceiued, if my thoughts intend
A satisfaction but in noble wayes.

*Ien.* S$^{r}$, my Master charged me, you should not haue so long an inter=view.

*Spr.* Beleeue it as I am a gentleman, I will not deale vnworthylye.

*Enter Peter.*

*Pet.* Wife my M$^{r}$ mistrusts you'l yeeld to that w$^{ch}$ is not fit for you to yeeld to, & hath sent me to bid you be an honest woman & carefull of his iewell.

*Spr*: If you had spoken softlye, you had shewed more wit, but proclaimeing yo$^{r}$ errand alters the case, & so get yo$^{u}$ gon or Ile pink yo$^{r}$ turkie grogram. *Drawes Ex: Pet:*

*Con.* Doe not yo$^{r}$ selfe an iniurye deare S$^{r}$
by being violent

*Ien.* Good M$^{r}$ Spruce begon, you see the times are dangerous, Scouts abroad & euill eyes vpon vs; but tis often, so; doe an old heauie vnwieldye gentleman a courtesie, & he'l say Woman I know you not; 'tis a hard case when a woman

659 *Scouts*] written over deletion, characters illegible

is faithfull yet suspected; another time, tempted to sin,
yet punishd for doing it; & 'tis a fine world, when a
master of a companye will reueale the secret of a trade.

*Con*: Sweet S$^{r}$ be pleased to take the councell she
Giues you I dare say, for yo$^{r}$ own behoofe,
A parting freind w$^{th}$ earnestnes expects
His freinds return; this hath not bene the first,
Nor shall it (w$^{th}$ heauens fauour) be the last
Day of o$^{r}$ meeting, & o$^{r}$ mutuall comforts

*Ien.* Giue me an earnest you affect my M$^{ris}$
And Ile indeauour any thing but being
Disloyall to her. *Giues her gold.*

*Spr*: This is the midwife

*Spr*: This is the midwife to most vndertakeings [FOL. 9a]
Let it be daintie handed now, & I shall euer praise it.

*Ien.* I am true as steele I warrant you.

*Spr*: Be you propitious too, or I am curst,
Th officious priests vnlock the temple dore,
But from the oracle comes the benediction,
For which, I kneele to you.

*Con*: Rise gentle S$^{r}$,
Cheare vp yo$^{r}$ selfe, & shake off sad despaire,
In hope the knots of this disturbed day
Precede the smoothnes of a happie age.

*Spr*: Let these imbraces then be prophecies
That o$^{r}$ affections shall outliue o$^{r}$ greefes,
That we shall meet, & part, & meet againe,
With touches easie as your gentle thoughts,
As now we doe, & then part no more.
But we must part, & heauie truth restraines
The comparison, from holding any longer. *Ex. Con: & Ienet*
Dick Crisp.

*Cris*: Here S$^{r}$.

*Spr.* Thou hast heard all?

*Cris*: Most S$^{r}$.

*Spr*: Should the old iade proue false now, for I dare not
mistrust the others puritye.

664 *will*] second *l* altered from *t*     689 *With touches ... thoughts,*] interlined

*Cris*: S$^{r}$ I am perswaded, M$^{ris}$ Ienet is but slipperye ware to deale w$^{th}$, yet I think I can tell yo$^{u}$ S$^{r}$ how she may meete w$^{th}$ her match.

*Spr.* Is thy genius so readie Dick?

*Cris*: yes S$^{r}$.

*Spr*: Giue me thy meaneing.

*Cris*: Then thus S$^{r}$, m$^{ris}$ Ienet for her own likelyhood of gaine, canot, when you please to desire it, denye you admission, though she may hinder or interrupt yo$^{r}$ conference; but S$^{r}$ you once entred, & I waiting on you, I'le offer you some of the confectioners com̄odityes, which you may w$^{th}$ a large com̄endacõn p$^{r}$sent to yo$^{r}$ m$^{ris}$, then I haueing certified you before S$^{r}$, the priuy marks of some confets w$^{ch}$ I will haue made purposely of *Nux vomica*, you may giue them to m$^{ris}$ Ienet, who haueing bene euer since she was thirteene both lico= rish, & insatiable, will accept them in hast, eat 'hem w$^{th}$ out further question, & im̄ediatlye fall down like an astonisht crow; then may you S$^{r}$, haue a coach readye, away w$^{th}$ yo$^{r}$ cariage, go to a place conueinent, fit yo$^{r}$ next actions to yo$^{r}$ further circumstances & so yo$^{r}$ humble seruant S$^{r}$. / .

*Spr.* Ingenious Dick! [FOL. 9b]
Old statists are but nouices to thee
for apt contriuement, great rewards are due
To thy inuention; if the sequell be
Grac'd w$^{th}$ success, thy vigilance & care
Shall feele thy Master loues thee; but alas,
'Tis not thy care, or my desires can do't;
My mistresses fauour, or all the hopes I haue
In her chast heats, or in her soft consent;
'Tis a continued series of degrees,
With out a broken step betweene, by which
I can ascend; I must haue all the hopefull circumstances
Twisted hard, & tied vp in one knot, to this assureance
My thoughts flie swift & high, & dare p$^{r}$sume
To merit in the confidence. *Ex. Sp. & Crisp.*

*Enter at the other dore M$^{ris}$ Mumble*
*& Sophia, w$^{th}$ a siluer tankerd ./*

711 *priuy*] interlined above caret 730 *haue*] interlined above caret

*Mum.* Giue me my vnckles legacie, this tankerd he gaue me by his will, good drink makes vs remember or freinds aliue & dead. *She drinks it off.* How should I ha done wth a great deale, that blow so much wth drinking this little.

*Sop.* The tankerd's a pretye draught forsooth.

*Mum.* I wench, but who can help it? we that are old must doe as we may; yet I ha known the day, when I haue drunk three of these of high countrye white to my mornings draught, & bene no fuller then needs must nether; & Ile tell thee the day too, it was the next morning after thy father died, tis a perilous alteracõn, for a woman to fall from three to one, & by reason of her infirmityes to be stinted of her drink.

*Sop*: you are not yet very weake forsooth.

*Mum.* I that's true, I can speake, or els farewell I; but my danceing failes me, my drinking you see decayes, two turkie eggs serue me now to breakfast, when I haue eaten heretofore seuen, besides cold red deare, fried clarie & lambstones, but thou sayst right, I can speake indeed.

*Sop.* I said you were not very weake forsooth.

*Mum.* No? thou seest I goe wth a staffe.

*Enter Godfrye :*

*Godf*: Mr

*Godf*: Mr Strife the lawyer is come to see you forsooth. [FOL. 10a]

*Mum.* Bid him come in Godfrye, bid him come in, *Ex: Godf:* but doe not tell him I goe wth a staffe, *throwes ye staffe away* a handkercher girle, me thinks my nose drops, & my lips are clam̄ie. *she wipes her mouth* *sings the next line to the tune of K. Arthur*

Now lawyer I defie thee doe thy worst.

*Enter Strife & Godfrye.*

A pretye good treble still, *Sophia*, pretye cleare, pretye cleare.

*Strife* I may wthout speakeing for fauour or affection, & wthout feare of haueing a writ of errour brought against my opinion con=clude so too, wth yor good leaue, licence, sufferance & ꝑmission I take possession of the prmisses *Kisseth her.*

737 *vs*] interlined

*Mum*: Sawcie knaue away, heare yo$^{r}$ m$^{ris}$ secrets, that she will impart to none but her councell?. *Ex: Godfrye*

*Strife*. And further hopeth that he yo$^{r}$ said seruant shall hold, occupie, possess & inioy the same.

*Mum*. you are a very learned man, M$^{r}$ Strife.

*Strife*. And haue free ingress, egress, & regress W$^{th}$out any let, hinderance, molestation, disturbance, interruption, or euiction whatsoeuer.

*Sop*. As this deponent verylye thinketh, as was written in the paper that lapt vp my tiffanye, you wooe like an ass.

*Mum*. What sayes she m$^{r}$ Strife?

*Strife*. She sayes the Arcadia is a better author then Littleton, & com̃ends S$^{r}$ Philip Sidnye, before my Lord Diar.

*Mum*. Nay it's a parills wench [..] but age will 'reaue her M$^{r}$ Strife .

*Strife*. Indeed I haue many times seene a wild yong man, after a yeares swing or two follow his studie close, & in conuenient time, turn a good student, I meane for a chamber practiser.

*Mum*. Ha'you so,? how say!

*Strife*. Euen so, may M$^{ris}$ Sophia in time.

*Sop*. Liue to see you sell yo$^{r}$ bookes, & turn a countrye atturnye.

*Strife*. A well wisher to yo$^{r}$ mother deserues more respect in law, trulye yo$^{r}$ vsage is not good in law.

*Sop*: You will not haue me leaue yo$^{u}$ forsooth?

*Mum*. As thou wilt Sophia, I haue not had a quame a great while, & now I dare venture my selfe alone w$^{th}$ a man; I would be loth to tell m$^{r}$ Strife an vntroth, or to couzen a gentleman w$^{th}$ a diseased bodye that comes to me in loue.

*Sop*: Indeed forsooth, you are too forward. *Whispers this & Ex. Sop. Strife.*

*Strife* Lyeing alone do's you much harme; it were farr more vsefull behoouefull, & aduantageous for you, to be vnder couert baron, the english of the french is to be maried forth with. [FOL. 10b]

*Mum*: You say true M$^{r}$ Strife, for then all the care will not lye vpon one single bodye.

*Strife* Then prouided allwayes, yo$^{r}$ mind be so setled conueighed & assured, as I hope you haue no cause but to think yo$^{r}$ promiss irreuocable, you may haue yo$^{r}$ husband, meaning my selfe, to follow yo$^{r}$ law busines w$^{th}$out a fee.

785 *Diar*] *a* altered from *e* 809 *promiss*] *i* written over corrected *e* 810 *law*] interlined above caret

*Mum.* I so; I may.
*Strife.* I will direct yo$^{r}$ seruants, & saue you the expence of meat
drink & wages to an ouerseer, bayliffe or stuart.
*Mum.* Reasonable well.
*Strife.* I shall receaue yo$^{r}$ rents for you, w$^{th}$out puting yo$^{u}$ to the
trouble of weighing yo$^{r}$ gold,, or fouling yo$^{r}$ fingers w$^{th}$ counting yo$^{r}$ siluer.
*Mum.* Then account to me for all yo$^{r}$ receipts.
*Strife.* So I shall be rather a seruant then a husband.
*Mum.* How? doe we differ allreadye?, then I see yo$^{r}$ greatest
aime is at my estate.
*Strife.* Not so, nether; for though you be old, yet I guess yo$^{u}$ are
wholsome, & I shall pay you all mariage dues, prouided
allwayes, vpon lawfull warning, & seasonable prouoca=
tion, not too sodainlye after meales, nor when I haue
store of clients at my chamber in an after noone.
*Mum.* These are very reasonable exceptions.
*Strife.* Besides if any scruple stick in yo$^{r}$ mind, Ile do the best
I can to cleare it; & for yo$^{r}$ estate, Ile make yo$^{r}$ will
when I see you palpablye decay, & so yo$^{u}$ may die the quieter.
*Mum.* Nay then farewell honest squire Spruce of *Norfolk* my first,
& Thomas Mumble of London merchant my second husband,
that would neuer tell me of death for feare of breaking
my heart, seldome comes a better. *Enter Thrifty & Peter.*
*Thrif*: Yes here comes a better, *Thriftye* the valiant, that come to
affront the lawyer, M$^{r}$ Contention, M$^{r}$ Strife, I should haue said,
Dare you p$^{r}$sume to be my riuall impudent!
*Strife.* I will lay claime vnto this gentlewoman; & proue my
title good.
*Thrif*: I tell, you tis as ominous, as for an Ins of court to breake
vp co͞mons in the middle of a terme; *suo sibi, suo sibi*,
how is it Peter?
*Pet. Hunc iugulo*
*Pet.* *Hunc iugulo gladio, S$^{r}$.* [FOL. 11a]
*Thrif*: Peter I acknowledge thee, 'tis so indeed good Peter; thou art
the better schollar, as I told you before.
*Strife*: I will not put this vp beleeue it S$^{r}$.
*Thrif*: Widow I rescue thee out of the lawes black phangs.

816 *trouble*] interlined above caret *gold*,] interlined above caret 835 *M$^{r}$ Strife*,] interlined above caret

*Mum.* A cup of voyding beare for m$^{r}$ Strife, a cup of voyding beare for the gentleman.

*Exeunt. Thriftye, Mumble. Peter.*
*Ex: Mr. Strife at the other dore*

*Fin Act ·2·*

*Act ·3·* /

*Enter Wild, Sophia.*

*Wild.* If w$^{th}$out scrueing yo$^{r}$ selfe into a posture of dislike, or an hipocriticall refuseing the affection of a man of resolue, when I know it is [a thing] most competible to yo$^{r}$ sex, (though a thing not so much worne) rather to accept, then to crye I heare you not; you can complye w$^{th}$ the proposition of one, that neuer affected complement, & knowes it is fan=tastick to vse it, I shall be readye to verifie the prouerb, by shortning the course of solicitation, w$^{th}$ a speedie closeing vp the match, & tyeing the knot.

*Soph.* Once I confess I saw you, when my brother
Gladlye inioyd yo$^{r}$ companye, & brought
You to my mothers' house, where that poore pittance
Which was made readie for her selfe, & vs,
you pleasd to accept, but had not any thought
you app$^{r}$hended such a worthines
In me, to vrge you, to this proposition.

*Wild.* Can you receaue a more firm assureance
Then mine own protestation vnconstraind?
Conceit first tooke me then, w$^{ch}$ I confess
Was worth the makeing much of; time the mother
Of truth did feed it; I perceiued it growing,
And pleasd in the particular degrees
Of augmentation, humblye now beg leaue,
My seruice may lie gentlye at yo$^{r}$ feete.

*Soph:* I wish it had a worthier place to rest in.
But yet restrain'd by filiall obligation, [FOL. 11b]
I dare not giue you any nearer wellcome
Then in a freindlye thought.

*Wild.* Then stay it sweet
But where it is, soft cherishing will blow
A willing spark into a lustie flame.
I'm blunt yet loue you, & if you should be angrie,

Perhaps there is abilitye in man
To cure that *atra bilis*; & I profess
My selfe a learnd phisician, whose integritye
Dare not delay yo$^{r}$ cure.
*Soph.* Soft hastie S$^{r}$,
you must giue mild p$^{r}$paratiues before
you offer stronger phisick.
*Wild.* As I would wish, thy first born child shall be
My eldest son, that I am resolud on.
*Soph.* Excuse me S$^{r}$, I pray be not so earnest,
for I haue two to please besides my selfe,
A mother & a brother, & vntill
Their free consents giue way to my desires,
My virgin answers must be negatiue.
*Wild.* Thou art the starr of prime dominion,
And I p$^{r}$sume their ioint resplendencie
Will warm by imitation, though below
In an inferiour circle,; yo$^{r}$ brother *Spruce*
And I, are so inwrapt in deare societie,
Nothing can shake that firmnes; & yo$^{r}$ mother
Will soone be wrought by him; my quick address
Shall beg his power to help my vndertaking,
The gods of mariage & of prossperous speed
*Hymen & Hermes* bring the designe to ripenes. [*Exeunt*].

*Enter at the other dore, Spruce leading Constance by the arme,* [*P*] *Crisp, & Ienet.*

*Spr*: Great things rise by degrees, & sodainess
In an ascent is rather a p$^{r}$diction
To ruin, then success; this moderation
Hath brought vs thus farr, w$^{th}$ a happie gale,
And still blowes faire
*Cris*: Those the musk, those the pearle; & those the amber S$^{r}$. [*giues*
*Ien.* The amber confets are good restorers, I pray [*Sp: confets*]
giue me some.
*Spr.* And not these onely, but a richer gift;
Weare this ring on yo$^{r}$ finger, & I shall

898 *mother*] *m* written over *b* 913 *Spr:*] written over deleted *Cris*: 914 *an*] interlined above caret 918 *Cris:*] written over deletion, possibly *Spr* 919 *Sp: confets*] *et* rewritten

Studie to thank you more; yo$^{r}$ glorious mistress

So farr

So farr out lusters all, I can p$^{r}$sent her, [Fol. 12a]
My admiration is my offering.

*Con.* Those com̃on wayes of seruice are of vse
Where the man wants perfection, & gifts
Are more successfull w$^{th}$ a chambermaid,
Then p$^{r}$ualent w$^{th}$ women of desert.

*Spr*: An eminence liues in yo$^{r}$ braue discern,
w$^{ch}$ I must reuerence

*Enter Wild.*

*Wild.* I haue not much outstayed yo$^{r}$ expectation
Pardon my rudeness Ladye, that I press
Thus sodainlye into yo$^{r}$ faire societie.

*Con*: Excuses are vnnecessarye, since
yo$^{r}$ freind bespoke yo$^{r}$ wellcome.

*Ien.* O the megram, the megram.

*Wild.* Pox the wood euill, is it not? the old beast hath the gid.

*Ienet turns round & falls downe.*

*Con.* O what ailes the woman?

*Spr*: No harme deare M$^{ris}$.

*Wild.* A little drunk, nothing els.

*Spr*: Ile tell you truth; that I might haue a free fruition of yo$^{r}$ deare p$^{r}$sence, my seruant skilld in simples did make these comfets w$^{ch}$ will stupifye & num̃ the senses, that the partie greeud will lie a time in such a strange distraction as she appeares, yet you need not feare, these partitions directed me w$^{ch}$ were for her.

*Con.* And will she take no hurt by being so?

*Cris*: No hurt at all, tis *nux vomica*, a simple they vse to catch

[*Cris*:] crowes w$^{th}$

*Wild.* Alas good buzzard, what a beastly thing is a woman drunk!

*Spr.* As you haue granted many humble suits
To me yo$^{r}$ seruant, so vouchafe yo$^{r}$ fauour
Once more, & that will make amends for all
The suffering, I haue born vnwillinglye;
Deigne me yo$^{r}$ p$^{r}$sence in some other place

929 *chambermaid*] first *a* rewritten; second *a* rewritten    931 *in*] *n* rewritten over deletion, now illegible

Then this, w$^{ch}$, you know, is so lyable
To danger, that we scarce can whisper safelye;
Ile take off all the doubts, you can oppose
By a kind of anticipation
You canot blame or question, this gentleman
Shall be companion of my seruice, till
You be perswaded no close priuacie
Can doe yo$^{r}$ ho$^{r}$ :
Can doe yo$^{r}$ honour wrong; consider [FOL. 12b]
How yo$^{r}$ ascent may giue extremitie
Of happines to him that honours you
Beyond expression; if disloyalltie,
Or tender of my satisfaction,
Aboue yo$^{r}$ virgin honour, durst attempt
By lustfull thoughts, to shame the heart they came from,
Iustice would not haue giuen me leaue to make
A feigned protestation, but powrd downe,
Im̃ediatlye, the sad reward of falsehood,
Sodaine vnlookt' for death, so to preuent
Successiue words from future periurye.
*Con.* You haue taken off
The colour of an opposition.
No sooner you exprest yo$^{r}$ own affection,
But you contended, (brauelye in yo$^{r}$ selfe)
To set a higher estimat vpon
My reputation, then yo$^{r}$ own delights.
Such a thing as mistrust, I'm not acquainted with,
The companye forbids, the qualitie
Of persons promise greater faithfullnes,
To which I giue a firm credulitye
Of being noblye vsed.
*Wild.* You're now set free.
W$^{th}$out the reach of an old midwifes eie,
At least a woman of as frequent trading. { *Ien: stirrs*
*Cris:* She hath some symptoms of recouerie
*Spr.* Let yo$^{r}$ deare mercie haue compassion
Vpon the man, whom neuer any influence
Of starrs till now inioynd to be transported
W$^{th}$ admiration of a womans maiestie.

The time giues licence, opportunitie
Stands as I haue implord, this gentleman
The witnes of the seruice I shall striue
To make a tender of; a coach at dore
Waits to receaue you, & a noble freind
Of mine, will giue you hospitable wellcome,
Not as you merit, but as he is able.
The place some few miles distant, & the passage
As free from danger[s], as the merchants wish
The way to th'Indies; please you set one foot forward
I will not
I will not take a greater boldnes on me [FOL. 13a]
Then to sustaine this arme. *Ienet rises & falls againe.*

*Cris*: She rises $S^r$.

*Spr.* Hast as you loue my being.

*Wild.* The more you stay, you are in the greater danger of being surprised, the amazed crow recouers.

*Con.* Then when you will goe on, propitious starrs, & you defend.

*Spr.* My seruice & that wish shall keepe you safe. / *Ex: oes*

*Ien: riseth, staggers & falls againe* *prot: Ienet*

*Ien.* Tis three howres since I drunk the muscadine, there is no remedie the other nap will do't.
*Offers to rise & falls againe.*
It will not doe, man or woman must yeeld to their betters
Muscadine & tosts I subscribe. *She sleeps*

*Enter Thrifty, Peter.*

*Thrif*: Peter.

*Pet.* $S^r$.

*Thrif*: How do's fame sing me abroad?

*Pet.* Conuinc't by truth, she now dares doe you right, & doth proclaime aloud in the eares of those that enuie you, you are discerning & impartiall.

*Thrif*: The spark of merit will not be hid in ashes; but yet except my selfe, there's not a man in a whole appareance at a sessions, that knowes how to distinguish busines, or to put proceedings in a method; if it were not for *Tullies par=*

1029 *Conuinc't*] *c* written over deletion, now illegible

*tem patria*, I think I should forsweare the bench, the habit of their ill language is so apt to corrupt mine, & the frequencie of their mistakes to seduce my vnderstanding into error, by their example.

*Pet*: How impertinentlye, yo$^{r}$ next neighbour, I meane on the left hand interrupted yo$^{r}$ wor:$^{pp}$ in yo$^{r}$ discourse of the necesitye of alehouses, & the moderne abuse of them; & then fell off w$^{th}$ a crye you mercie, trulye I mistooke you.

*Thrif*: Tis an ordinarye thing for such a fellow to talke much, & think he speakes wiselye, when by his tittle tattle he makes himselfe ridiculous in the face of his countrye; & but that custome lessens the sense, these men are burdens which a shoulder vnaccustom'd would be sore to support, but the

vulgar thank=

vulgar thankfully smile at not being sensible of their own opp$^{r}$ssions. [Fol. 13b]

*Ienet riseth & comes toward them reeleing.*

*Pet.* My wife come to bid yo$^{r}$ wor$^{p}$:$^{p}$ wellcome home.

*Thrif*: Housekeeper! how fares all at home, did you obserue remem=ber & execute.

*Ien.* Things goe not so well as they should, forsooth.

*Pet.* That's true, for thou goest as if thou wert drunk, goe so well as they should, quoth she! they goe ill fauouredlye, for thou reelest euery step, as I am vertuous S$^{r}$, she is drunk, ꝑfectly drunk, an't like you.

*Thrif.* Fye, fye, say not so.

*Pet.* Nay tis w$^{t}$hout all scruple S$^{r}$. indeed wife things go not so well as they should, tis confest they doe not.

*Ien.* S$^{r}$, I acknowledge my fault, but canot restore you yo$^{r}$ child.

*Thrif*: How ! *She weeps*

*Ien*: S$^{r}$, I was made drunk, & till now did not recouer, & my imꝑ=fections being wrought vpon, my yong m$^{ris}$ was stoln away.

*Thrif*: Why Peter. *He chafes & turns round about.*

*Pet.* Here S$^{r}$.

*Thrif*: Peter, I say, as I told you before.

*Pet*: At yo$^{r}$ worships elbow, S$^{r}$.

*Thrif*: O Peter, thy wife is a thing that is not worth my furye,

1036 *forsweare*] *wea* written over illegible characters

though heretofore, she hath allayed my heat.

*Pet.* S$^{r}$?

*Thrif*: As I told you before, stole away doest thou say?

*Ien*: Too true, I assure you S$^{r}$. [*She kneeles*

*Thrif*: Stand vp, stand vp, I hate all outside wor$^{p}$, I am no idol, & thou knowest, I am no Saint; stole away still, you say?

*Ien.* Yes indeed, S$^{r}$.

*Thrif*: Then a warrant for a priuie search Peter, & when the warr$^{t}$ is gone out, wee'l inquire the names of the parties that are to be lookd after.

*Pet.* Not to displease you, S$^{r}$, I think their names would be more properlye known first, els you giue direction to looke you know not whom.

*Thrif*: As I told you before, passion transports me in the course
of iusticiarie
of iusticiarie proceedings, but thy memorie inables thee to [Fol. 14a]
be recorder of a town corporat. Nay as I told you before it was impossible she should be true to her master, that would cuckold her husband when he was writing in the next roome, this I know to be true of mine own knowledge.

*Pet*: O goodnes defend S$^{r}$.

*Thrif*: As I told thee before, Peter, 'twas onelye w$^{th}$ me; but to giue thee satisfaction, I bequeath thee this tufftaffata ierkin, & w$^{th}$out more expostulation accept it, as a requiteall an=swerable to thy loss, & a right worshipfull recompence.
[*giues Peter his ierkin.*

*Pet*: I am content S$^{r}$, but me thinks I feele bunches rising here, I pray looke I think you may see 'hem w$^{th}$out spectacles.

*Thrif*: Vpon my worshipfull word the biting of a gnat. Now must I lay by my familiaritye, & excercise authoritie in the seat of iudicature. [*Goes into the chaire:*
Woman, woman, how write you yo$^{r}$selfe?

*Ien.* An't please yo$^{u}$ S$^{r}$, the right worp:$^{tt}$ Iustice Thriftyes housekeeper.

*Thrif*: Hum, That sounds scuruilye, & the cadence is incongruous.

*Ien.* Some fauour I beseech you S$^{r}$ for old loue.

*Thrif*: Woman I know thee not, Iustice is impartiall, & must not take acquaintance of the face of an offender, though she be

1102 *familiaritye*] curved line above first *a*    1106 *Hum*] interlined above caret

a Ladye of parts. But who is t you suspect made you drunk?

*Ien.* Ether a great mornings draught to yo$^{r}$ wor$^{ps}$: health, or els
the confets M$^{r}$ Spruce gaue me, of so strange an operation.

*Thrif*: Set down m$^{r}$ Spruce principall.

*Pet.* Tis done S$^{r}$.

*Thrif*: Who accessaries, assistants, aiders, or comforters; speake woman.

*Ien.* M$^{r}$ Wild forsooth, & Crisp M$^{r}$ Spruces man, they were in
fault, & I beseech you consider it.

*Thrif*: Woman I tell thee as I told thee before, that for the p$^{r}$sent
thy fault onelye appeares before vs; & being once w$^{th}$in o$^{r}$ cog=
nizance, the eares of iustice must be deafe to the cries of ye guiltye

*Pet.* One word, for my wife S$^{r}$, I beseech you.

*Thrif.* Fellow, fellow, as my clerk I know thee, but as one that speaks
for the delinquent, I am vnacquainted w$^{th}$ thy face, her
fault is w$^{th}$out p$^{r}$sident, & she must be punished accordinglye,
Fye a drie nur
fye, a drie nurse, be drunk when she should looke to her charge. [FOL. 14b]

*Ien.* S$^{r}$ I was ouercome by vnlawfull meanes.

*Thrif*: I, so crye all yo$^{r}$ women offenders, in truth it was my hard
chance to be ouercome; thy fault is w$^{th}$out example, & thou
shalt haue a punishment of mine own deuise, to see the
ignorance of o$^{r}$ forefathers, that knew not how to fit a
mulct to an offence, how improperlye haue they set
women behind the cart, & then whipt 'hem inhumanlye,
I will therefore alter the practise abate the whipping,
haue thee & thy confederats if they may be come by draw
a cart along the streets on a solemn day, & this is yo$^{r}$
iudgem$^{t}$.

*Ien.* Good S$^{r}$.

*Thrif*: Take her away sententiouslye rebuk't,
When those are spared, should be seuerelye vs'd,
Mercye mistakes, & iustice is abusd ./. *Exeunt ./*

*Enter Wild, Sophia.*

*Wild*: Fresh hopes w$^{th}$out mistrust did shine vpon
yo$^{r}$ brother, & his mistress; he deliuerd
This letter to my charge; sweet, open it,
And if you haue a competent proportion

1115 *comforters*] curved line above second *o* 1122 *Thrif.*] speech prefix straddles lines 1122 and 1123; drawn line indicates its placement at 1122 1143 *Fresh*] curved line above *e*

Of loue to answer his that there salutes you,
I need no intercesso$^{r}$, & yo$^{r}$ smiles
Shall stand respectiue paralells to his
Rendring yo$^{r}$ seruant happy.
*Enter M$^{ris}$ Mumble, & Godfrye.*
*Sop.* My mother, S$^{r}$.
*Mum.* Another suiter Godfrye
*Godf*: He's too yong forsooth.
*Mum.* Out rascall, ouerthrow the likelyhood of propagation!
Am I so old? I pray ask my midwife of the abilitye of
my bodye. |*Enter Constable & officers*
*Const.* That's the man, app$^{r}$hend him.
|*Enter Thriftye & Peter.*
*Thrif*: That's he the principall accessarie, & accessarie principall.
*Pet.* yo$^{r}$ wor p$^{'s}$ ith'right, he did abet as you haue oath for it.
*Wild.* One speake
*Wild.* One speake at a time, though you & yo$^{r}$ clerk doe not vse [FOL. 15a]
it, the reason of this violence to me?
*Thrif*: O simple fellow, a delinquent examin a iustice of peace,?
gooder, & gooder as I told you before; he that asks me a
reason, Ile cõmit him for that; take him away.
*Sop*: for my sake S$^{r}$, haue pitye |*Ex. Constable, & officers w$^{th}$ Wild.*
on that gentleman, when you were yong perhaps a suppliant
Of meaner parts might haue p$^{r}$uailed w$^{th}$ you.
*Thrif*: I grant it Lady, but now my needle stirrs the trembling
point toward this wholsom coole North pole, & feares
a yonger torrid [yonger] zone like wild fire./
*Mum./* What sayes he, what sayes he?
*Thrif*: I say, youth stands ticklish vpon the sere; put down but a
button; snap; it goes off like a stone bow, or a gun new oyld.
*Mum./* Trulye & so it do's.
*Sop*: S$^{r}$, w$^{th}$out a more continued cruelltye,
Release the worthye gentleman, my word
Shall be his baile, if you will, please to take it.
*Thrif*: Will you be bound bodye for bodye?
*Sop.* Had I desert to be an equall price
for his deare safetye, or might ransom him

1173 *a yonger*] *yonger* interlined above caret

With tender of that brittle thred of life
My safetye hangs on; nature was not more bounteous
In lending me my breath, then I should be
forward in retribution of that debt,
To gaine assureance of his p$^{r}$seruation.

*Thrif*: Then Ladye, let yo$^{r}$ mother but say ye word, & tis done.

*Mum.* I thank you hartylye good m$^{r}$ Thriftye.

*Thrif*: Trust me m$^{ris}$ Mumble as I told you before, things must
be as they may, when they can be no otherwise; & though
authoritye be hot when it is incenst, yet Iustice is euer=
coole ith' latter end of a day; Let m$^{r}$ Wild be set at large,
doe you heare me there?.

*Pet*: yes S$^{r}$, it shall be done *Exit Peter.*

*Mum.* Then Godfrye get in, & bid Bridget make the bride bed
readye as soone as may be, no hast but the sooner the
better, my phisician assures me the dog dayes are
past, & now it is wholesome.

*Thrif*: Thou shalt feele, & confess it widow. *Ex Oēs.*

*Fin: Act .3. / .*

*Act . 4.* [FOL. 15b]

*Enter Catch & Snap. two theeues.*

*Catch.* Barr hanging, & the Empero$^{rs}$ territories are but a yonger
brothers portion to o$^{rs}$, & compared w$^{th}$ vs, the great
Mogull is not yet out of his wardship.

*Snap.* Pish we are free born, & come to o$^{r}$ estates w$^{th}$out sueing
a liuerye.

*Catch.* That's the reason, that if we giue any of the officers wine
or a breakfast, they'l accept it of grace, not exact it
as debt.

*Snap.* True & you may call any of 'hem knaue, & their [guylt] guilt &
yo$^{r}$ independence, will free you from being told you mistake
the man, but stand close I heare companye..

*Enter Spruce, Constance, Crisp w$^{th}$ a chest of bottles.*

*Spr.* Come come my fairest charge, when we shall be
Blest w$^{th}$ a quick ariue at that wisht place,
Which an howers trauaile more will bring vs to;

1206 *compared*] *c* written over erasure 1213 *guilt*] interlined above deletion 1216 *Constance*] *ta* written over erasure

And consum̄ation of o$^{r}$ nuptiall ioyes
Shall by the fullnes of solemnitye
Giue vs the freedom, to express o$^{r}$ thoughts
In liberall action, changeing staru'd conceit
Into the high fed execution
Of things, w$^{ch}$ ayerie words haue not the power
To make vs vnderstand, yo$^{r}$ own beleefe
Will, like yo$^{r}$ selfe, make a confession
free & ingenious.

*Con.* for all those heauy sufferings w$^{ch}$ I
Haue bene exposed to, this hower makes amends.

*Catch.* I am not taken w$^{th}$ such amorous courtship.

*Spr.* As for yo$^{r}$ ease & recreation, you pleased to leaue the coach, & make the surface of this blest place to thanke you, for depressing those humble blades of grass, which rise againe as gratefull subiects, when their soueraigns hand takes off the yoke of seruitude; so now vouchafe at my intreatie to receaue a spoonfull of restoreing wine, that's mixt w$^{th}$ spirit of pearle & amber.

*Con:* Ile not refuse any thing you com̄end.

*Spr.* Dick Crisp, powre out some wine, but w$^{th}$ so soft a motion that the spirits loose not their strengths.

*Catch & Snap discouer themselues.*

*Catch.* Sirrha first deliuer you what you haue about you. *to Crisp:* [FOL. 16a]

*Crisp.* Truly S$^{r}$, I haue nothing but this chest of strong waters, &, my box of instruments w$^{ch}$ I surrender. *Runs out.*

*Snap:* Gentleman & Ladye, the old saying, need breakes stone walls teacheth you what to doe. *they offer to lay hands on Sp. & Con.*

*Spr.* you will not be vnciuill?

*Catch.* We must, & therefore we will; no disputing, we are resolud.

*Spr.* I am ashamd two things so noblye born, as will & resolution should be so much abused.

*Snap.* A man can hardlye grow fat w$^{th}$ eating stones, or a mans land ladye be paid w$^{th}$ cryeing excuse me, S$^{r}$, time has bene we haue thought it scuruie to goe w$^{th}$ o$^{r}$ haire vnpowderd, & bene of opinion, that a twelue penye ordinarie or a cooks shop would make a man stink w$^{th}$ looking into, or lowsie

1227 *confession*] curved line above *e* above caret  1232 two short, faded, angled lines '//' in left margin  1247 *offer to*] interlined

if his cloke should but sweep vpon the stall; but now S$^{r}$,
euery man for his being, that he may eat; & tis not time to
come a new oath, to sweare 'tis for my reputation; these
were things once, but now S$^{r}$, I assure you, the bellye that
is hungrie will not chide the tailer for makeing clothes out
of fashion; a man must be, before he can be a gallant, one
is essentiall, the other but a kin to circumstance, I am
plaine w$^{th}$ you, you must change doublets w$^{th}$ me.

*Catch*: And breeches w$^{th}$ me S$^{r}$.

*Spr*: Shall I secure this Ladye then?

*Snap*. All but her clothes & iewells.

*Con*. Take all good gentlemen, onelye spare my life.

*Catch*. O that it were as it had bene, that I had such a little
duck as this, to vsher to a play, or wait vpon to the stillyard,
but the more cross are the starrs, tis not so happie; yo$^{r}$
iewells, sweet Ladye yo$^{r}$ iewells,:

*Spr*: Her iewells! how you slaue? flye for yo$^{r}$ safetye; these
two barking currs, Ile quiet w$^{th}$ as much facilitye as if
I were at any sport I loue. *Spruce drawes vpon them*

*Catch*. Are you so gamsom? what sence haue you for this? *shewes a pistoll*

*Snap*. Or this? *shewes his pistol*

*Spr*. Nay then I do beseech you, flye as fast
As yo$^{r}$ abilitye can help you forward. *Giues them a iewell*

*Con*. As you haue bene compassionate to me,
Shew equall mercye to this gentleman.

*Catch*. We are not safe o$^{r}$selues, this place doth lye
Obnoxious

Obnoxious to diuersitye of dangers, [FOL. 16b]
And is liable to more then vs of this condicõn;
If you desire to saue yo$^{r}$ life away.

*Con*. Tis a hard choice
To die in present, or to looke for death
W$^{th}$ in an howers space; perhaps a minuts;
farewell, the best, the noblest gentleman
That euer had misfortune by a woman;
If you escape, consult w$^{th}$ euery path
Which way I went, Ile write my sad complaints

1292 *escape*] *s* rewritten

Vpon some heauy tree that stands alone,
And in a hand that none can read but you. |*Exit.*

*Spr.* I am insensible, els I had perceaued
The power that left me; you may exercise
All the tormenting violence you please,
Or cruelltye can think of; my disasters
Haue past the height of their extremitye,
And dulld my app$^{r}$hension, that I canot
Perceiue iniurious vsage.

*Catch.* Off w$^{th}$ yo$^{r}$ doublet. Come. |*Spruce puts off his doublet.*

*Snap.* yo$^{r}$ breeches too S$^{r}$.

*Spr:* I beseech you gentlemen

*Catch.* Emptye yo$^{r}$ buttond pocket then & we will fauour you so much as to dismiss you. |*Opens his pocket & giues them mony.*

*Spr.* As I loue vertue, there is all I haue,
& if you will but retribute one peece
to beare a sad nights charges, if kind fate
shall make that honourd gentlewoman (you saw
part in such discontent) & me to meet againe,
Ile owe you double thanks

*Catch.* What a braue thing it is to be the better man, brother, what say'st?

*Snap.* Thou knowst, what want will driue a good man to, & there is no such vexation as to meet w$^{th}$ a mans wench, & want monye to pay for her supper. |*Giues him a peece.*

*Spr.* As I liue; that religious innocent is my betrothed wife

*Catch.* Giue him a Iack for thou knowest
None but Spankers, & Lawrells will pass in o$^{r}$ companye.
fare ye well S$^{r}$.

*Spruce goes one way aside, they another ./*

*Snap.* Come share; share.

*Enter 3 other theeues, Careless, Killman, Dingthrift.*

*Care.* Halfe o$^{rs}$, or stand.

*Catch.* Theeues amongst o$^{r}$selues, nay then tis time to leaue the trade. |*They fighting Exeunt, & let fall Spruces doublet.*

*Spr.* Then

*Spr.* Then I hope this is a good portent [FOL. 17a]

1319 *Spr. As I . . . wife*] interlined 1323 *aside,*] interlined above caret

of future safetye, when a man is sad
Tis sin to cherish melancholye; raise
Thy low brought spirits, seeke thy louelye mistress,
W$^{th}$ eyes of inquisition, & a mind
prompted w$^{th}$ zealeous earnestnes; but O
My spirits faile me, when I do repeat
Her name, & am debarrd the looking on
So braue an obiect. I must sacrifice
My actions to her, as well as my resolues.

*Enter Crisp.*

*Cris*: How doe you S$^{r}$?
*Spr.* O thou stinking coward.
Leaue me in such extremitye?
*Cris*: My loss is most S$^{r}$, for I haue lost my box
Of siluer instruments, my iointed siringe too.
*Spr.* All the black curses that haue bene produc'd
By inuocation light on thee & them.
Where are the theeues?
*Cris*: Gone S$^{r}$, I had not stirrd els.
*Spr.* Art thou sure?
*Cris.* Am I sure, I am here S$^{r}$! I peept as long as I could see
a man, before I crept out of the hollow tree.
*Spr.* Plague o' yo$^{r}$ creeping; but where's the Ladye *Constance*?
*Cris.* Trulye you pose me now S$^{r}$, all my drift was but to saue
yo$^{r}$ wor$^{ps}$ barbers skin, who should haue trim̃d you if I had
bene killd?
*Spr.* Oh thou dull slaue, respect mortalitye,
And let an angell slip thy obseruation!
Humanitye mistakes, I greeue not as I am bound,
I must accom̃odat my sorow,
Not as the customarye mourners weep
That whine for fashion, but as the noble thing
I am depriu'd of claimes of right. Crisp come hither.
Goe looke the woods, & euery formall tree
That giues thee salutation, take by th' hand,
And ask it how it do's.
*Cris.* Why I beseech you S$^{r}$!
*Spr.* If the tree make a leg, wilt not thou put off thy hat?
*Cris.* That I shall S$^{r}$.

*Spr.* Except yo$^{r}$ master be, at the same time, likelye to be robd,
& then you'l run away.

*Cris:* O I beseech

*Cris*: O I beseech you S$^{r}$; I remember it to my greefe. [FOL. 17b]

*Spr.* And you haue seene a tree make a leg, I know.

*Cris.* Vpon yo$^{r}$ wor$^{ps}$ word I take it S$^{r}$.

*Spr.* Very good S$^{r}$. you are a freind at need; you'l tell a lye
to make yo$^{r}$ master merrye, or sweare a thing because his
wor:$^{p}$ sayes it; you that would leaue me then, Ile turn
away now.

*Cris*: No I beseech you S$^{r}$.

*Spr.* Yes truly S$^{r}$.

*Cris*: Deare S$^{r}$ yo$^{r}$ pardon, & trye my seruice once more.

*Spr.* Then heare yo$^{r}$ charge, & w$^{th}$ such care & speed
As thou wouldst vse to get thy pardon signd,
If, for want of it, thou wert to die to morow,
Goe range the woods, leaue not a shepheards' boy vnquestiond,
That can but count his sheep, let not a milkmaid
Escape thine inquisition, & all other meanes
Be earnest in, whereby I may be satisfyed
Of Constance, or her fortunes.

*Cris:* I goe S$^{r}$, theeues miss me, & I am happye. [*Ex. Cris:*

*Spr.* How many thousand hipocrites do shed
Their teares that a compassionat spectator
May say I am sorye for 'hem? & as many
Do drye their eyes, when there's no looker=on
To be a witnes of their suffering,
Esteeming it a gross absurditye
Not to weep, when anothers sad occasion
Inuites 'hem to't for companye; but I
Need not a cue to prompt me, my calamitye
Hangs not vpon the approbation of
Another mans opinion; here it lyes
That scorns a fiction, when a reall torment
Contends w$^{th}$in, the heart must yeeld, or breake;
Ile seeke a healeing remedie, tis she
That by the elixer of her pure appeareance
Must make me liue; thou feminine maiestie
Looke on me w$^{th}$ thy splendor, that I may

Haue one occasion more to thank kind nature
for lending me mine eyes. *Exit.*

*Enter King of shepheards & 5 other shepheards.*

*King.* for my yeare & in o$^{r}$ sheep walks, Pan was neuer a more absolute king, nor is there a better gouernd com̃on wealth in Arcadia then o$^{rs}$.

*1Shep.* Nay, that's w$^{th}$out all peraduenture.

*King:* you are all

*King.* you are all of that mind? [FOL. 18a]

*2Sh.* All, all, let him die of the rot that is not.

*3. Sh.* I am of that mind too, but I dare not say so, for feare of displeaseing my landlord; for he saies, his wor:$^{p}$ being a Iustice keeps the beggers in a more formall subiection then the king of shepheards his vnder dealers.

*King.* Who? thy land lord?

*3. Sh.* yes his good wor:$^{p}$, king.

*King:* I will rebuke him p$^{r}$sentlye, & shew thee, what a poore ordinarye thing a Iustice of peace is, that studies statute yet dares not doe, as the law leads, for feare of displeasing the great man, his next neighbour, that tooke in the cõmon.

*4. Sh.* O, I know who that is.

*King.* I, but when yo$^{r}$ king speakes, you must neuer say any thing, but good, or well spoken, or admirable, or so, neuer disturb him; but crye, king goe on, or bless o$^{r}$ gouerner.

*1 Sh.* The king sayes true, of a certaine.

*King.* Then subiects be content, when you are required, to put yo$^{r}$ cambrells quietlye into the hooke of restraint; struggle not, when yo$^{r}$ kings dog catcheth by the eare, though he pinch it quite thorough, or make the blood come; be not vnwilling to receaue the pitch brand of distinction, though the iron be so hot, it make yo$^{r}$ buttocks blister; are yee content?

*All.* Yes, yes, very well content

*King.* Then dig a shepheards table, against the wenches bring o$^{r}$ flawnes, & sillybubs, they'l geere vs, if we be tardie.

*The Shepheards dig a shepheards table.*

*Enter Musitians.*

*Mus.* Very good musick, an't please you.

*King.* How dare you trauell that are rogues by th' statute!

*Mus.* A very good new song, if you'l heare it.

*King.* Songs! no I thank you, we i'the countrye take songs to be parlous things, they say such as you haue bene whipt for songs

*Mus.* That was for singing the cleane contrarye way; we will not do so, but you shall heare a staff or two on liking.

*Enter 6 countrye wenches w$^{th}$ prouision.*

*King.* Tib, & thy companions wellcome to th'hill, strike musick.

*They sit down, & eat, Musick playes.*

for thy wellcome Tib, thou shalt heare a sonet of mountain poetrye, keep time lads, & minstrells play you on yo$^{r}$ fiddles.

*King sings.*

*King sings .* [Fol. 18b]

*While harmless shepheards watch their flocks,*
*In mirth & iollitye*
*The sounding ecchoes of the rocks*
*Increase their harmony*
*No troubleous or tormenting care*
*Can eclipse the geniall day,*
*Appointed to receaue the faire*
*Inuiters of their play.*
*Tib.*
*1 Sh.* *Madge.*
*2. Sh.* *Bess.*
*3 Sh.* *Kit.*
*4. Sh.* *Iil.*
*5. Sh.* *& Kate*
*All.* *Lasses of the downe.*
*Euery one of which*
*Sticks a flower, & takes a stitch*
*In the king of shepheards crowne.*

*King.* *We need no Ladies of the Court,*
*That laugh their Lords to scorne,*
*Who to afford their seruants sport*
*Make their husbands weare the horne.*
*Our homely wenches of the downes*
*Are more delightsome farr,*
*And weare their comely pleated gownes*
*More handsom, & these are*
*Tib.* [*&c*]

*1 Sh.* *Madge.* *as aboue.*
*King:* *We need no citye tradesmens wiues*
*They looke too much in glasses,*
*And lead themselues, such Ladyes liues*
*They make their husbands asses.*
*Our sweet breathd wenches looking glass*
*Is a cleare open spring,*
*Where euery one suruayes her face*
*While her sweet heart doth sit & sing*
*Tib.*
*1 Sh* *Madge. &c.*

*Enter Crutch & his wife w^th^ Constance.*

*Crutch.* Certainlye

*Crutch.* Certainlye I know not the way. [Fol. 19a]
*Con: [wife]* Nor you old mother?
*Cr.wife.* Whence come you gentlewoman?
*Con:* It would abide a long discourse to tell you
All the sad chances I haue vndergone
And by what vnexpected miracle
I light vpon you.
*Crutch.* And whither would you?
*Con.* To any village that is but hospitable,
But yet the place I most desire to goe to,
Is M^r^ Wellcom's house.
*Cr:wife* You were lapt in yo^r^ mothers smock, that is his shepheard.
*King.* father *Crutch*, wellcom will you take part?
*Crutch.* Thank you hartylye, you are king this yeare?
*King.* for want of a better father *Crutch*, you know places of trust & co᷉mand are not allwayes put into the hands of men of desert, as for example, the Constable of o^r^ town this yeare is a foole; the next Iustice of peace is a I marrye is he, the Sheriffe of the Countye a man of good clothes, & the Lord of the mãnor an elder brother.
*Con:* It seems you know 'hem all.
*King.* I haue my walks from this hill to that dingle, from that bush to the other thick thorns, if a sheep leap out of order, my dog giues him a fetch againe, & my whistle a recall,

1487 *Sh*] placed before erasure 1497 *Sh*] placed before erasure 1501 *Con:*] altered from *Cr.wife*

& this is my life, & my master (w$^{ch}$ is strange now adayes)
is an honest gentleman that neuer inclosed, M$^{r}$ Wellcom
of Wellcom hall, but I pray you gentlewoman, will you
sit down & tast.
*Con:* Not a bit I thank you.
*King.* Away w$^{th}$ these things then, & quicklye to yo$^{r}$ dance.
*Con:* May you not from yo$^{r}$ sportfull iunketing
Spare me yo$^{r}$ meanest shepheard boy that knowes
The way to M$^{r}$ Wellcoms, I will recompence
His paines w$^{th}$ thankfull tender of reward
To make his labour more insensible.
*King.* If you would haue a guide to lead you thither
Ile do't my selfe if please you; father Crutch,
I pray supplye my place, you haue bene good at it.
*Crutch.* Nay fekins Ile not leaue the gentlewoman till I see her
at the hall.
*Con.* Old mother you I hope will go along too.
*Cr: wife* Yay marry will I gentlewoman.
*King.* Then Tib my queene, do you see things in order, [FOL. 19b]
I will conduct this gentlewoman.
*Con.* I owe a great debt to the king of shepheards
That at the sodaine importunitye
Of an vnknown stranger, he'l be wrought to leaue
His sport, & faire societie.
*King.* O Lord forsooth, tis not so much worth,
Ile be proud to be yo$^{r}$ gentleman vsher. *Ex. King. Con. Cr: & his wife*
*They dance & Exeunt oes*
*Enter Spruce at the other dore ./*
*Spr.* Mortalls suruiue disasters, that their sense
May know a difference; did we not liue to beare
Mischances, the impartiall hand of fate
Were conscious of iniustice, benefits
Are p$^{r}$parations to calamitye,
And if a man haue liu'd so happyly
To share in ioy, 'tis Iustice like proportion
Of greefe should some times take vp other thoughts,
To make him know how corresponding poize

1530 *Con:*] four short light angled lines in left margin 1552 *their*] *t* corrected from *s*

Giues euen motion, when the skye's serene,
To sayling ships, & ballanceth their great
Vnwieldye bulks in a tempestuous sea.
Should death succeed my wish, the expiration
Would taxe my selfe esteeme, should I deplore
My life, it were less manly then to slight
The troubles that attend it; he that bewailes
His being, is not so meritorious
As one that smiles at introduced ills,
The last hath hope, the other in despaire
Weeps like a child in such a base deiection,
As if things were impossible to rise
To any height of mending; application
Names me infected, diuersitye of wayes
To resolution humblye yeeld themselues,
To my disturbed app$^{r}$hension,
And bid me choose, how can I make election
The oracle replyeing doubtfullye,
Or bring oblations to an emptye shrine
With confidence, when I know the saint is absent
To whom I owe my pilgrimage? if I die
By mine own hand, the action is ignoble
And she will haue a seruant fewer, if
I liue my life will be vnprofitable,
Vnless
Vnless a firm assureance of her being [FOL. 20a]
In safetye make it vsefull. I haue obserud
And prosecuted obseruation
W$^{th}$ such a curious search, there's not a tree
In all the forest, that hath bark vpon it
And that bark capable of impression
I haue not bene at councell w$^{th}$; iust starrs
Beare witness she com̃anded it, & can
Obseruance supererrogate, & suffer
for being too inquisitiuelye sedulous?
*Enter Crisp.*
Better or worse, speake out.
*Cris:* May't please you S$^{r}$.
*Spr.* I shall be pleased as thy short relation

Offers me cause
*Cris:* Did you not see the shepheard S$^{r}$?
*Spr.* The shepheard? I haue neuer seene a man,
Or els thought all men trees, since the faire queene
Of beautye did com̃and me to examine
The barks of those mine eye should fall vpon.
But didst thou see a shepheard?
*Cris:* Yes S$^{r}$, a shepheard of signification
Yo$^{r}$ vnckle Wellcoms shepheard.
*Spr.* O hadst thou met
The ministeriall angell, that's designd
To wait on *Constance*, & receaued intelligence
from him of her safe being, 't had bene punctuall.
*Cris:* Let not my faithfull seruice be receiued
W$^{th}$ incredulitye, like *Cassandra's* councell,
And I will raise yo$^{r}$ wonder, & vnfold,
More then yo$^{r}$ hopes can probablye suppose,
Maruells yet truths, for wonders all are true.
*Spr.* Thou strik'st me dumb, my diligent attention
Shall not intrude an interruption,
So to produce my satisfaction sooner.
*Cris:* Then S$^{r}$ beleeue me, as yo$^{r}$ known experience
Hath found me euer seruiceable, I met
Yo$^{r}$ vnckle *Wellcoms* shepheard coming from
His masters house, (the place w$^{ch}$ you intended
To bring yo$^{r}$ mistress to) whither, he sayes,
He did conduct her safe.
*Spr.* My *Constance* safe?
*Cris*. As you or I S$^{r}$.
*Cris.* As you o$^{r}$ I S$^{r}$, & will there remaine [FOL. 20b]
Vntill the inquireye of a day or two
Doe satisfye her, whether it be likelye
To heare of you or no.
*Spr.* If this be true,
It is the fairest morning after raine
That euer shone vpon a wearied man.
*Cris:* If it be false, the shepheard is the most

1602 *Spr.*] two short light angled lines '//' in left margin 1618 *Spr.*] two short light angled lines '//' in left margin

Perfidious slaue that euer did conuerse
Wth beasts of gentle temper.

*Enter Mr Wellcome & his shepheard*

*Shep.* That's the man Sr, the gentleman I know not.
*Spr* My honord vnckle.
*Well:* My dearest nephew,
To giue you verball wellcome, were to take
Away the freedom, & proprietye
You haue where I am master, but I bring you
That wch is worth yor knowledge, yor faire mistress
Is at my house, & safe.
*Spr.* Sr it is the onelye sublunarye good,
Next to her sweet fruition, I beseech you,
Giue me leaue to hast to that.
*Well.* Tis cruelltye to keepe you long asunder,
Yor loue is so reciprocall, for when
She heares you nam'd, the claps her hand vpon
Her heart to keep it downe, & yet 'twill rise,
And leap vp toward her eyes, & neuer be
It selfe at rest, or reconciled to them,
Vntill they ease it, wth their gentle teares.
*Spr.* Most orientall drops!
O, that I had 'hem in a diamond box,
They would eclipse the lustre of the stone
And make it seeme a conterfet; Good Sr,
Let vs away, think, you were once inflamd,
Allthough you canot think how I desire.
*Well:* Ile goe as farr as an old man can towards it,
And yet I know, & must confess, it is
The curse of weakenes, & of old age too,
To wish, what is impossible to doe. *Exeunt.*

*Fin . Act . 4 .*

*Act . 5 .*

*Act . 5 .* [FOL. 21a]

*Enter Thrifty, Constable, & officers. Peter & Ienet.*

*Thrif:* Officers.
*Con:* Sr.
*Thrif:* Harness yor flanders mare, & dispatch the execution.
*Ien.* I beseech you Sr, examin fully whether I were in fault

alone, & if I had partners let them suffer w$^{th}$ me.
*Thrif:* After the sentence is past, there is no reuocation, Ile
first punish the fact & then examine the busines.
*Pet.* I humbly do beseech you S$^{r}$ forgiue, for others instigation
did vrge her to 't.
*Thrif:* As I told you before, though there be no consideration to
be had of the persons, yet there is of the men, & thou knowest
by my mariage I am to haue relation to 'hem [all] all.
*Pet.* My ill memorye betrayes me S$^{r}$.
*Ien.* S$^{r}$ as you haue euer found me seruiceable,
forgiue my fault, & spare the heauy punishment.
*Thrif:* Woman as I told you before, the punishment of offenders
is the phisick of a diseased com̃on wealth, I cõmit you
to these men, & they shall giue you a glister. Peter stay
you to see whether the beast draw gracefullye. ⌊*Ex. Thriftye*
*Pet.* Deare wife it is but one bout for his worp$^{s}$ satisfaction, &
another in *terrorem feminei generis*, a thing most
necessary, & compound w$^{th}$ yo$^{r}$ memorie not to twit you,
a quarter of an hower ends yo$^{r}$ vexation.
*Ien.* Husband I disclaime thee, neighbo$^{rs}$ I call yee all to wit=
nes, besides his want of breeding, his disposition is ill,
& [besides] he is a fellow of a very loose conuersation. Stand
by to see yo$^{r}$ own flesh derided.
*Pet.* O wife, if I haue a wart vpon my hand that vexeth me,
blame me not if I make an vnction of pig's blood, or rubb
it w$^{th}$ marygold leaues till I bring it down; & if an ill
humor thrust out an offensiue bunch vpon my forhead,
shall I not seare it w$^{th}$ a cauterizeing touch of correction
to take away the excrescencye. Come executioners do yo$^{r}$ office.
⌊*They set her to the cart.*
Vertuouslye borne, wert not too frequent, for husbands to
ask their wiues forgiueness, I would crye thee mercye.
*She drawes the cart ouer the stage.* *Exeunt oēs.*
*Enter Wild & Crisp.*
*Wild.* What Crisp, returnd w$^{th}$ yo$^{r}$ aduenture?
*Cris:* Not so S$^{r}$, but pretye faire for the game.
*Wild.* Are you yet

1689 possible end-stop at end of line, though the mark is positioned between the lines, slightly above the *y* in *Thriftye* in the next line's stage direction

*Wild.* Are you yet vpon vncertaintyes? [FOL. 21b]

*Cris:* The truth is S$^{r}$, my M$^{r}$ is maryed, but not willing the world should take notice of it, till the old gentleman be appeased, & to that purpose, has dispatchd me w$^{th}$ this lre to my old M$^{ris}$, intreating her to get m$^{r}$ Thriftyes good will.

*Wild.* Tis very good reason she should, for he has got hers I am sure, & she protests the lyeing w$^{th}$ a man of qualitye has strangelye betterd her heareing

*Cris:* I do not app$^{r}$hend you S$^{r}$.

*Wild.* M$^{r}$ Thriftye has maryed m$^{ris}$ Mumble, that's the English on't, & so the reconciliation will be made w$^{th}$out opposition.

*Cris:* That followes not by yo$^{r}$ fauour S$^{r}$, many hug & bill before they're maried, & the first night once past (when they thought to know more then they did, & indeed look'd for more then was there to be found,) they fall to brawling & scolding, & wish they might neuer see nor feele one another againe, that you would think mariage had some strange magick in it, to sweare one thing & presentlye doe another.

*Wild.* If all do so, then haue I a faire peece of work in hand.

*Cris:* The storye is sad S$^{r}$, but it is oft known a truth, most men are so serued, & there's scarce a [maried] man of my acquaintance that dare brag he is excepted.

*Wild.* Howsoeuer, if it be but to perfect my vnderstanding, Ile haue one bout in the honorable state, & yo$^{r}$ yong M$^{ris}$ *Sophia*, is the woman I am to venture on.

*Cris:* Mariage vpon mariage, tis pitye the world should be vnpeopled, or things at the best grow worse, for not being taken in time, but S$^{r}$ I am trusted, & canot be at quiet till I haue disburdend my selfe faithfullye; I must needs to my old M$^{ris}$, wilt please you to goe S$^{r}$. |*Exeunt*.

*Enter Peter & Ienet.*

*Pet.* Nay wife, now I see there's no hope of you, I giue you for a lost woman, yo$^{r}$ bodye & yo$^{r}$ mind are both irrecouerable, the wildfire is gotten so hot into yo$^{r}$ bones, & all yo$^{r}$ whole bodye become a lump of proud flesh, that nether corasiue nor pultess will coole the inflamation; & for yo$^{r}$ mind, af=

1733 *maried*] interlined above caret and deleted 1744 *no hope*] *no h* written over mark 1745 *irrecouerable*] *i* altered from *c*

flictions doe not make you vnderstand yo$^{r}$ error, nor dandling or philters incline yo$^{r}$ affection to me yo$^{r}$ deserueing husband.

*Ien.* Marry gep pen & inkhorne, breed a boy to a man, & he'l leaue you when you haue most need of him, euen mine own case; you canot denye, but that I was yo$^{r}$ first raysing,
& from
& from a poore scrieueners boy, aduanced you to be yo$^{r}$ masters [FOL. 22a]
clerk, that no man makes suit to him, but he cryes Peter shall I grant it, & yet now you dare be so impudent as con= tend w$^{th}$ yo$^{r}$ foundress; thy ingratitude will be thy iust condemnation.

*Pet.* O thou ꝑfect Xantippe, but that thou wantst a chamber= pot, though it be thy shame yet it is my greefe, that thou darest thus reuile thy head.

*Ien.* Sirrah, Sirrah, if rep$^{r}$hension will do no good on you, beating shall. *Shewes a ropes end.*
off w$^{th}$ yo$^{r}$ hat, & giue me my due respect. *Puts off his hat*

*Pet.* How a healthfull bodye will be taken down w$^{th}$ a disease, I quake w$^{th}$out an ague.

*Ien.* Peter my handkercher, goe back Sirrha, I haue lost,
*He goes back & fetcheth it.*
What a great comfort, a well tutord child is to his parents, take me by th'arm, so. *Ex. he leading her by the arme*

*Enter M$^{r}$ Thrifty, M$^{ris}$ Mumble,*
*M$^{r}$ Wild, M$^{ris}$ Sophia & Crisp.*

*Wild.* S$^{r}$, here's a messenger come from Kit Spruce, w$^{th}$ his seruice to you, & a letter to his mother.

*Thrif:* He dos well, freind Richard?

*Mum.* O how do's Kester, how do's my boy?

*Cris:* If he haue not a countermand, he'l sodainlye be here forsooth, I am sure he's on his way, his m$^{ris}$, m$^{r}$ Wellcome & his wife & more of good fashion w$^{th}$ him. This letter is to you forsooth.

*Thrif.* Is *Constance* but his m$^{ris}$ yet?

*Cris.* No an't please you S$^{r}$, onely they sit both in an end of the coach; & dare not goe further w$^{th}$out yo$^{r}$ good will.

*Thrif.* I here giue it him before witnes, as I told you before.

1754 *from*] curved line above *o* 1761 *though*] written over *thou* 1765 *hat &*] partially stroked through

*Mum.* Loue, pray looke vpon my letter. |*He looks vpon the letter*
*Wild.* They sit both in an end of th'coach, you say?
*Cris:* Yes S$^{r}$.
*Sop:* So shall you sweet heart, for a moneth after you are maried
sit ith' coach by me, & then some other Spruce fashionist shall
take that place, & you ride on horseback ith' raine.
*Wild.* As I loue you, I am in yo$^{r}$ debt for that
*Mum.* Richard I referr you to my husband for answer, it ⟨..⟩ is his day
of com̃and by couenant of mariage.
*Thrif.* Freind *Crisp*, tell yo$^{r}$ m$^{r}$, as I told you before that I vnderstand
he is
he is maried, & his hast hath giuen me no offence; [FOL. 22b]
*Cris.* Yo$^{r}$ wor$^{pp}$ good health S$^{r}$. |*Ex. Crisp.*
*Wild.* Now my day, I beseech you, S$^{r}$.
*Thrif:* What sayes *Sophia*?
*Wild.* Tis fit indeed S$^{r}$, she should haue the choice
Of that night, wherein she must sustaine a loss
Will make her smile to beare.
*Thrif:* Content, content, daughter for now you'l giue me leaue to
call you so, name the time yo$^{r}$selfe.
*Sop:* Maids are but suffered to conceiue their wishes,
And not to bring them forth till they be maried.
*Thrif:* And you are a maid too m$^{r}$ Wild I am sure? what say you?
*Wild.* My wishes wait on hers, & can be crownd
onelye in her desires.
*Mum:* Two maids, two maids, vpon my life, two maids.
*Thrif:* A well met couple; may yo$^{r}$ first child proue a wise man,
Trulye I doubt it, the prouerb needs no com̃ent.
*Mum.* Very well put, husband, very well put.
*Thrif:* Then, no more adoe, but thus, as I am bound by my place
to be a pacificall reconciler of differences, so I desire you
may ioine w$^{th}$ all conuenient speed, & leaue the time to
yo$^{r}$selfe & yo$^{r}$ daintie deare; yo$^{r}$ thanks I expect in the
wedding gloues, as I told you before.
*Sop:* They shall fit yo$^{r}$ hand S$^{r}$, take my word;
And I hope w$^{th}$in a yeare to haue a child,

1793 *for*] curved line above *o*  *it* ⟨..⟩ *is*] long smudge extends above line from deleted characters, now illegible  1801 *indeed S$^{r}$*] partially stroked through

Shall, w$^{th}$ a smile, express the mothers thanks./

*Enter Peter Ienet following & beating him.*

*Ien.* Nay you hipocriticall rascall, Ile teach you to look
vpon me, in all companyes alike, if you will be com=
plaining, Ile giue you cause to complaine.

{ *She espyeing Thriftye, & the rest, throwes away the*
*rope, looks demurely, & makes cursye.*

*Pet.* Now S$^{r}$ at the later end of a day, I beseech yo$^{r}$ fauour to
yo$^{r}$ old seruant Peter, for since I performd yo$^{r}$ com̃and
to see iustice done vpon this feminine siner, she hath
hurried me, as if I were one of her charr women.

*Wild.* My fellow sufferer accused?

*Ien.* I beseech you heare me, this fellow that for respects
known to yo$^{r}$ wor$^{pp}$. I haue long vouchafed to call husband,
is of a very ill life, profuse at the ale house, a niggard to
me, spends all abroad, yet denyes me necessary cherishing,

though I

though I demand it; & then all his sence is, *Ienet* I canot [Fol. 23a]
doe as I haue done; O S$^{r}$, I canot doe as I haue done is
the womans miserie, I canot doe as I haue done, is that
w$^{ch}$ made the alderman breake.

*Thrif:* Nay it appeares plainly, as the Sun at noone dayes, or the
kings arms in the Shire hall, that whensoeuer a ma=
ried man pleads, he canot doe as he hath done, he intends
to goe less, & cheat w$^{th}$ a non ꝑformeance; Tis a thing,
I confess, I neuer durst doe.

*Ien.* No S$^{r}$, yo$^{r}$ free nature did euer scorn it.

*Thrif.* O Ienet, how tender is thy sense of my venerable reputa=
tion, I am bound to releeue thee, both in want & plentye.

*Pet* And what shall I do, I beseech you, S$^{r}$?

*Ien.* Marry get a pen that writes fuller, sweet husband,
& not scrible scrable, like a boy that runs crooked
though his paper be ruled w$^{th}$ two lines; I say againe,
get me a text pen that writes fuller, & neuer draw a
stroke, but crye, wife do's it please you?

*Pet.* Would you haue me suffer this too?

*Thrif:* Vnderstand me Peter, yo$^{r}$ patience is now most congruous,

1840 *done is*] *e* rewritten    1844 *whensoeuer*] *o* altered from *e*

since what yor wife said, came in as a coincident, as I told you before, & not participating of the bodye of the busines, as you erroneouslye conceit it.

*Ien.* Husband, husband, we trouble his wor:pp & Ile giue you a touch for all; the more you striue, the weaker you will grow, yor way is to be quiet, & that will get you strength, & when you haue it to be industrious towards yor wife & that will make her countenance you in companye, & loue you in priuate.

*Mum.* How well mirth do's between husband, & wife!

*Thrif:* Admirable well wife, as I told you before; come, come, shake hands you loueing couple, you feigne passion, but haue none; shew anger, but yet neuer knew it; redden but to make yor blood thin, & to obserue the phisicians rule, *ad ruborem tantum*; where suspition ha's bene conceiued let it die; if a fault haue bene, beleefe shall be most officious to make you think there was neuer any such thing; two mariages haue bene; Mr Wild, & yor daughter, wife, are to make vp the third, besides you Peter & Ienet, shall be new maried ouer againe, when my son Spruce, & daughter come home, the first night
we three

[FOL. 23b]

we three couples will lie all in a chamber together, & you Peter & Ienet in the truckle bed, as I told you before; sack possets shall goe a begging, & by vertue of those that are eaten ouer night, euery woman shall next morning run after her man, as a hen pigeon after treading followes her cock, & in her amorous language calls him, Tom, Tom, Tom ti tom, Tom ti tom, Tom ti tom, Tom ti tom.

*He runs round, as a pigeon turns first one way, then another.*

*Enter Godfrye.*

*Godf.* Sr, I haue according to yor direction attended vpon the leads, & euen now, discouered the companye, I think you expect.

*Thrif:* Familye, let's away, the more state we keep, the more ob=serueance we attract, & though we are not proud, we will not be com̃on, nor vouchafe familiaritye wthout solicitation, as I told you before. *Exeunt Oēs.*

*Enter Mr Wellcom, Mris Wellcom, Mr Spruce, Mris Constance, Cruch, & his wife at the other dore.*

*Cr: his wife:* Wearie, wearie, wearie.

*Const.* Alas good woman; & how doe you, father Crutch?
*Crutch.* Limp after the progress, a little foundred too
*Cr: his wife:* I was vp betimes, & am a little sleepie now, doe you not vse
to bait in a whole dayes iournye,? pray is it not the
fashion, to say you are not wearie when you are, or
will being wearie make one a gentlewoman?

*Enter Crisp to them.*

*Spr.* What satisfaction, can yo$^{r}$ iournye giue my doubtfull thoughts?
*Crisp.* Things goe rarelye well S$^{r}$,
Iustice Thriftye has maried yo$^{r}$ mother S$^{r}$, & sweares as
he is a man put in trust w$^{th}$ a diuision, he was neuer angrie,
& you shall be as wellcome to him as muscadine after
brawn, or sack before supper.
*Well:* And how did my sister take the sodaine newes?
*Crisp.* She laught as she read the letter S$^{r}$, & euery second word
that past betweene M$^{r}$ Thriftye & her selfe, was, Heark yo$^{u}$
loue, or pray sweet heart obserue, they play like conyes,
& toy, as if they were but coming to that, which they were
twentye yeares agoe abridg'd of, by imperfection of vnable
bodyes.
*Spr.* May it but turn to my aduantage, &

I shall

I shall applaud w$^{th}$ voluntarye suffrage [Fol. 24a]
Those toyeings, w$^{ch}$ their liberall conceit
Is plenteous in, but worn abilityes
Constraynedlye forbeare, & be as ioyfull
As their sense seems delighted.

*Enter M$^{r}$ Thrifty, M$^{ris}$ Mumble, M$^{r}$ Wild, M$^{ris}$ Sophia, Peter, Ienet & Godfrye, fowre countrye men & women, w$^{th}$ presents.*

*Thrif:* Peter.
*Pet.* Here S$^{r}$.
*Thrif:* Put the busines in a forwardnes, as I told you ⟨.⟩ before,
that my complete salutation may bid the strangers well=
come, & as the course is when you haue concluded the matter,
then ask what my plesure is in the busines.
*Pet.* I shall S$^{r}$, come good folks attend, yo$^{r}$ name busines, &
abiding place.

1932 *as the*] *e* altered, possibly from *y*

*Count:m* I, an it shall like yor good worpp: Mr Parchment.
*Pet.* Fye, fye, speake softlye. *Countrye folks whisper, & Pet: writes*
*Thrif:* A prime part of magistracie, as I told you before, consists
in laying by passion, & disclayming partialitye, yet there are
many cautions to be obserued in vouchafeing clemencie
to the penitent, & extending seueritye to the incorrigible &
refractorye; now obserue yee me, *consideratis considerandis*
& as I told you before, you are all most heartylye wellcome,
brother, sister, son, daughter, wth all the implements, [of]
accouterments, & necessarye dependencies of yor longtailed
traine. *He salutes them & kisseth the women.*
*Spr.* Except my bold aduenture hath wth=drawn
yor fauour from these noble furtherers
Of my designes, they may wth rightfull claime
Challenge a freindlye wellcome.
*Thrif:* O Sr, as I told you before, I being sworn to keepe the peace
to the best of my power, should breake my oath if I should
nourish malice in my breast, especiallye agt those that are
made of my kindred by the coniunctiue work of matrimony
I, I say againe, be forsworn euidentlye forsworne; & you must
obserue, as I told you before, we are neuer to be forsworne,
except it be, in matters of moment, or busines of small con=
sequence.
*Spr.* I will not prss the rules wch iustice gouerns by,
But thankfullye
But thankfully acknowledge you vouchafe [Fol. 24b]
The beauteous outside, yor iudiciall robe
Denyes to guiltye men, whose sad reuerse
Propheticallye, speakes their condemnation.
*Thrif.* O Sr, condemn! I acquit you as I am right worp:full,
my noble freinds, please yorselues wth discourse of yor
own finding; the countrye attends, & dexteritye in ex=
pedition, (which I am famous for,) gets the good will
of a mans neighbors, & sometimes (as I may tell you, in
priuat,) a dish of chickens, wch are more easylye receaued
then bred, though corn be neuer so cheap.
*Thrifty turns from them to the suters.*

1965 *full*] interlined above caret

*Well.* S$^r$ we shall attend yo$^r$ plesure. *Mr Wellcome & his com= pany talk priuatlye.*

*Thrif:* I shall desire you to speake low, my loueing brother, because the com̄on peoples obserua= tion is too apt to be led away, & their attention is most necessarye, by reason of the diuersitye of heads I am to speake vpon, & their dullnes of app$^r$hension.

*Well* I crye you mercye S$^r$.

*Thrif:* Now Peter you know, I am to take where you leaue, therefore express thy conceit, & inform me how farr you haue waded into the busines.

*Pet* An't shall please you S$^r$, for yo$^r$ better vnderstanding & yo$^r$ more orderly proceeding, here is a breefe of the businesses, expressiue & directorie.

*Thrif:* To w$^{ch}$ partie doth this busines belong?

*Pet.* I haue accom̄odated their busines to the persons, & plac'd their suits in yo$^r$ wor$^{ps}$: paper as they stand in order before yo$^u$.

*Thrif:* O thou necessarye epitomiser of tediousnes, how most auxiliar thou art, to a man ꝑturbd w$^{th}$ multiplicitye of affaires, I conceiue thee to mine own aduantage, & approue thy sufficiencie as I told thee before

*Pet.* S$^r$, an it like yo$^r$ good wor$^p$:$^p$ these two brought you the p$^r$sents.

*Thrif:* We must not take notice of that openlye, but manifest o$^r$ acceptation, by fauouring the parties, & expedition accor= ding to their own desires, but this is *misterium authoritatis*, & so vnderstand it, *Speakes this aside.*
Then thus Peter, *Points to the paper, & then to the parties.*

*Pet.* Miraculouslye app$^r$hended S$^r$, as I perceiue yo$^r$ sentence intends to be punctuall.

*Thrif:* Then not a word more to any, but to this good woman,
that lookes
that lookes so sadlye; for yo$^r$ comfort; yo$^r$ daughter shall [FOL. 25a]
escape whipping, & yet the parish keepe the child, where it was nether got, nor borne.

*1 Coun:wom.* Bless your good wor$^p$:$^p$ a poore p$^r$sent for yo$^r$ wor$^{pp}$:

*Thrif:* 'Las neighbo$^{rs}$, I neuer take bribes, but because you shall not take it vnkindlye, Ile accept yo$^r$ good will.

1994 *you*] interlined above caret

*1 Coun:wom:* O fare fall you S$^{r}$, mine are but fowre chickens forsooth, but should haue bene fiue, if the fift had not run away, & I wanted companye to catch it, but I hope it may be a hen in time, & a dam̃ of more chickens for yo$^{r}$ wor$^{ps}$: table.

*Thrif:* Run away doe you say, the fift chicken run away?

*1 Coun:wom.* Yes ant please you, to my greefe, but my good will was not wanting, to shew my thankfullnes to yo$^{r}$ wor$^{pp}$:

*Thrif:* Nay if that be a hinderance, that you could not catch it, Ile send a man or two to help to catch that extrauagant chicken, that chicken that respects not, but runs away from authoritye; & onely for yo$^{r}$ reputation that are the giuer, & not for my com̄oditye that am the receiuer, as I told you before, I would be loth yo$^{r}$ gift should be but fowre, when yo$^{r}$ meaning was fiue, or haue yo$^{r}$ p$^{r}$sent niggardlye, when yo$^{r}$ mind is bountyfull. What did he flye for't? [C] catch the chicken again, & bring it.

*1 Coun.wom* At yo$^{r}$ wor:$^{ps}$ good plesure.

*2 Coun:wom.* A couple of fat capons for yo$^{r}$ wor$^{p}$:$^{p}$ they are cleane capons, as yo$^{r}$ wor:$^{pp}$ may ꝑceiue by the length, of their tailes.

*Thrif:* Trulye neighbo$^{rs}$ as I told you before, I am sorye it is my hard chance, to be of so famous a merit, to extract out of my sufficiencie, w$^{ch}$ is insubstantiall, & lyes in the fancie, so great a proporcõn or, if you will, such a number of gratuityes.

*1 Coun.wom.* The countrye is happie in yo$^{r}$ wor$^{ps}$: neighbourhood.

*Thrif:* That we vnderstand as I told you before, & shall neuer be willing to hide those parts, w$^{ch}$ nature & art haue bestowed to the benefit of the republique, Peter you see my strangers expect my returne, haue my neighbo$^{rs}$ to the butterye, my little butterye in the parlour.

*All.* Long life to the founder. *Exeunt Peter & Countrye people.*

*Thrif:* My noble freinds.

*Thrif:* My noble freinds, Let not I beseech you my life be had in contempt, who am thus forced to descend to keep order in a Countrye; nor doe you think erroneouslye, my procee= dings are preposterous or corrupt, when mine own abilityes tell me, [FOL. 25b]

2021 *not*] interlined above caret    2032 *or*] interlined    *if*] *i* altered from *o*    2046 *or corrupt,*] interlined above caret

they are regular, & im̃aculat; I must fit actions to oc=
casions, & vary my language as my company; I haue
drunk wine w$^{th}$ poets, & small ale, & milk distilld, w$^{th}$
those that haue the stone; I can be as graue as a phi=
losopher, & foole amongst boyes & women; I say, No man
outfooles me, & tis a great point [partt] of wisedome to foole
discreetlye, some great men haue bene [are] p$^{r}$ferrd by't; I can
talk as bawdylye as a midwife, & againe, pinch in my
words, w$^{th}$ as little a mouth, & as great shew of p$^{r}$cisenes,
as a citisens wife, that vseth allom water for contraction.
When my neighbors come before me, you see, I am able
to vnderstand, & answer 'hem; their chickens stand for
hierogliphicks, & their capons secure their persons, as
the geese did the Capitoll. 'twas plaine in the womans
case whose daughter had the bastard; & thus I leap
from the lowest step to the top of gouerment,
As soone, & easylye, as a squirell climbs a tree;
This is part of my Cronicle, which I will haue p$^{r}$serued
In manuscript, till the printers be at more lesure.
My good freinds, I haue made you stay too long,
I will requite yo$^{r}$ patience, in yo$^{r}$ wellcome.

*Wild.* I take the boldnes in the name of these
Yo$^{r}$ worthye visitants, to confess they think
Their wellcome, (as yo$^{r}$ free intention
Will haue it,) noble; & because I am,
Vrg'd by mine own concerns to beg yo$^{r}$ fauour,
That my ioyes may be, as full, as my desires,
Pardon a yong man earnest, whose extreme
Is but a temperat medieocritye,
If you weigh the gale he sailes w$^{th}$, in the ballance
Of charitye & iustice.

*Thrif.* M$^{r}$ Wild I perceiue yo$^{r}$ day of mariage lies still in
yo$^{r}$ mind, yet, you know, I gaue you free libertye to
choose yo$^{r}$ own day S$^{r}$.

*Wild.* Yo$^{r}$ faire leaue giuen, irreuocable vowes
Tied the internall knot, but sensible
of the defect

2052 *point*] interlined above deletion 2053 *discreetlye*] *r* altered from *e* *haue bene*] interlined over deletion above caret 2080 *choose*] *c* rewritten

Of the defect a ceremonye hath [Fol. 26a]
Which is not grac'd w$^{th}$ store of companye,
We did restraine the outward complement
Of mariage, till the dayes solemnitye
Might be full w$^{th}$ the p$^{r}$sence of those freinds,
Whose wisht returne renders vs sensible
How greeu'd their absence was, but still
For the time submit to you.

*Thrif:* How are those men blest, that haue but the discerne to
know where merit lyes, & can giue an awfull respect to
magistracie, when that reuerence euer comes home,
w$^{th}$ a duck i' the mouth, as I will now make it appeare
to you. Had m$^{r}$ Wild, my now allmost son in law, ruffled
for his mistress, I had by my place caused the contempt
to haue bene recorded, & proceeded in discretion; but now
I must goe on cleane contrarye; &, in another way, send
a warrant for my neighbors to come to his wedding,
Which must be sodaine, & were it not that you
Haue bene so long deteind, w$^{th}$ lookeing on
The progress to this end, we should intreat
Yo$^{r}$ p$^{r}$sence at the mariage, which will be
Complete in all things but yo$^{r}$ companye. *Ex.* $\overline{\textit{Oes}}$.

*Fin. Act. 5* ###

2084 *a*] rewritten